Crowell Publications in History
KENNETH M. STAMPP
Advisory Editor for American History

The Crowell American History Series
JOHN HOPE FRANKLIN & ABRAHAM S. EISENSTADT, *Editors*

Morton Borden
UNIVERSITY OF CALIFORNIA, SANTA BARBARA

Parties and Politics in the Early Republic, 1789-1815

Thomas Y. Crowell Company
NEW YORK
ESTABLISHED 1834

For Jess and Sally, who sharpened the pencils

EDITORS' FOREWORD

It is a commonplace that each age writes its own history, for the reason that man sees the past in the foreshortened perspective of his own experience. This has certainly been true of the writing of American history. The purpose of our historical writing remains constant: to offer us a more certain sense of where we are going by indicating the road we have taken in getting there. But it is precisely because our own generation is redefining its direction, the way other generations have redefined theirs before us, that the substance of our historical writing is changing. We are thinking anew of our direction because of our newer values and premises, our newer sense of how we can best fulfill the goals of our society, our newer outlook on the meaning of American life. Thus, the vitality of the present inspires the vitality of our writing about the past.

It is the plan of the *Crowell American History Series* to offer the reader a survey of the point of arrival of recent scholarship on the central themes and problems of American history. The scholars we have invited to do the respective volumes of the series are younger individuals whose monographs have been well received by their peers and who have demonstrated their mastery of the subjects on which they are writing. The author of each volume has undertaken to present a summation of the principal lines of discussion that historians of a particular subject have been pursuing. However, he has not written a mere digest of historical literature. The author has been concerned to offer the reader a sufficient factual and narrative account to help him perceive the larger dimensions of the subject. Each author, moreover, has arrived at his own conclusions about those aspects of his subject that have been matters of difference and controversy. In effect, he has written not only about where the subject stands in historiography but also about where he himself stands on the subject. And each volume concludes with an extensive critical essay on authorities.

The books in this series are designed for use in the basic course in American history, although they could be used, with great benefit, in advanced courses as well. Such a series has a particular utility in times such as these, when the traditional format of our American history courses is being altered to accommodate a greater diversity of texts and reading materials. The series offers a number of distinct advantages. It extends and deepens the dimensions of course work in American history. In proceeding beyond the confines of the traditional textbook, it makes clear that the study of our past is, more than the student might otherwise infer, at once complex, sophisticated, and profound. It presents American history as a subject of continuing vitality and fresh investigation. The work of experts in their respective fields, it opens up to the student the rich findings of historical inquiry. It invites the student to join with his older and more experienced colleagues in pondering anew the major themes and problems of our past. It challenges the student to participate actively in exploring American history and to seek out its wider reaches on his own.

John Hope Franklin
Abraham S. Eisenstadt

CONTENTS

ONE

The Contributions of Federalist and Republican, 1789-1801

PROBLEMS OF A NEW NATION

"Be of good cheer," Gouverneur Morris counseled his fellow Federalist, Alexander Hamilton. "My religion steps in where my understanding falters and I feel faith as I lose confidence. Things will yet go right but when and how I dare not predict." Sectional jealousies, cultural cleavages, economic rivalries, all had to be resolved. The nation in 1789, one scholar has writ-

1

ten, "was the scene of an indigenous, deeply rooted, conflicting pluralism." Could the problems inherent in pluralism be surmounted for the sake of national unity and progess? Americans identified themselves largely by their local attachments. Could they learn to "think continentally?" Many Antifederalists had occupied positions of power in the state governments. They had fought hard, even bitterly, to block ratification of the Constitution. Would they swear fidelity to and serve the interests of a superior sovereignty? Americans' distrust of centralized government was part of their British legacy. The House of Representatives, after the Constitution was in operation, reprimanded James Madison for using the suspect term "national." Could Americans make federalism work? Their inheritance was revolutionary. Could they practice moderation? Could they find the magic balance between liberty and order? No less an issue than the future of republicanism depended upon the outcome.

The new Constitution, conceived in Philadelphia during the summer of 1787, was grounded in the concept of popular rule. But could the people be trusted? Much depended upon the nature of the emerging American character. Used with moderation and wisdom, the Constitution could become an instrument for securing the liberties won in the American Revolution. Used without restraint or republican spirit, its opponents claimed, the same Constitution could become a vehicle for despotism. Morris was not the only American whose hopes were wracked with doubts. The obstacles to maintaining a successful federal union seemed formidable.

Still, without demeaning the accomplishments of the Founding Fathers, their problems were not as formidable as they believed or liked to depict. Antifederalists dissented from the view that conditions in the late 1780's were critical. "All the powers of rhetoric and arts of description," complained Melancthon Smith, "are employed to paint the conditions of this country in the most hideous colors. We are told that agriculture is without encouragement, trade is languishing, private faith and credit are disregarded, and public credit is prostrate." Most scholars have long accepted and propagated the Federalist gospel that the Constitution rescued the nation from impending anarchy. Recently, for example, Clinton Rossiter (*1787: The Grand Convention,* 1966) has concluded that "Congress [under the Articles] was already falling when the Framers gave it their famous push." Other scholars, while admitting that difficulties existed, have denied that the nation was at the point of collapse. "Such a picture is at worst false," writes Merrill Jensen (*The New Nation,* 1950), "and at best grossly distorted." All such judgments are comparative. Consider the following:

1. The British still possessed the northwest posts in violation of the peace treaty of 1783. The Spaniards controlled New Orleans and capriciously permitted or restricted trans-shipments of American produce. Both instigated Indian attacks; both attempted to entice frontiersmen, sometimes with striking results; both wished to contain the westward expansion of Americans. Any policies the United States might adopt to settle these issues were bound to cause internal disputes. However, neither England, Spain, nor any other European power threatened America in 1789. As Patrick Henry told the Virginia ratifying convention, it was to the interest of Europe to remain on peaceful terms with the American states. "God has so separated us by an extensive ocean from the rest of mankind," wrote a Bostonian in 1788, "it would be impossible while we retain our integrity, and advert to first principles, for any nation whatever to subdue us."

2. Revolutionary war debts were largely unpaid, and arrears of interest by 1789 had increased substantially. England treated the United States with disdain, and refused to grant the infant nation a treaty of commerce. New international markets for American produce were harder to develop than Thomas Paine had once predicted. Nevertheless, the United States was rich in human and natural resources, and few could doubt its

vast potential. The Constitution, moreover, was launched during a period of economic recovery. The nation was emerging from the post-revolutionary depression which had thwarted the operation of the central government under the Articles of Confederation. The new government was linked to prosperity. Ratification of the Constitution stimulated a wave of optimism, even of exuberance. In more practical terms, ratification resulted in an increase in the price of Revolutionary War obligations: a positive sign of confidence.

    3. The very failure of the Articles, the scorn of England and the indifference of Europe stimulated Americans to prove that they could fashion an effective federal system. Marked historical consciousness—intrinsic in all great revolutionary movements—caused them also to realize that a second failure might well result in sectional fragmentation. Further, the vehement factional animosities which had accompanied the debates over ratification all but evaporated once the Antifederalists were faced with a *fait accompli*. Virginia, New York, and North Carolina Antifederalists continued to agitate for a second national convention. Several newspapers continued to print prophecies of disaster such as a military king, aristocratic domination, or an army of excisemen "to bit our mouths with massive curbs." Yet, as Thomas Jefferson informed his good friend, the Marquis de Lafayette, in April, 1790, "The opposition to our new Constitution has almost totally disappeared."

    Almost all historians have remarked on the phenomenon of good feelings which characterized the immediate post-ratification period. "Indeed, after its organization little more is heard of the party of opposition," wrote Woodrow Wilson in his famous book, *Congressional Government*. "They disappear so entirely that one is inclined to think in looking at the party history of that time, that they had been not only conquered but convinced as well." Madison's quick and clever action in drafting a series of constitutional amendments fulfilled the Federalists' campaign pledge to enact a Bill of Rights without compromising the work of the Founding Fathers. Some Antifederalists, such as William Grayson of Virginia, were less than pleased with Madison's proposals which affected "personal liberty alone, leaving the great points of the Judiciary, direct taxation, etc., to stand as they are." Nevertheless, the Bill of Rights quieted the fears of many Antifederalists and helped to persuade the recalcitrant state of North Carolina to enter the union. Last among the thirteen states, Rhode Island ratified the federal compact in May, 1790.

In retrospect, and by comparison, few twentieth century nations escaping from colonial bondage have started out under more auspicious circumstances than did the United States under the Constitution. India, for example, has been plagued by bloody religious and even linguistic conflicts, food shortages, and foreign invasion. African countries have had to contend with ancient tribal hostilities, national illiteracy, appalling poverty, frequent insurrections, insufficient capital, and economic backwardness. The United States in 1789 could hardly be described as a "have not" nation. It is true enough, as Seymour Lipset has commented (*The First New Nation,* 1963), that "many incidents . . . revealed how fragile the commitments to democracy and nationhood really were" in the early national period of American history. But one might also argue that American hypersensitivity to the danger of tyranny was in itself an effective barrier to such a development.

It is also true, as James Madison once said, that the fundamental task of the government was to unite "the minds of men accustomed to think and act differently." The United States was an economically diverse country. Northern and Southern customs and mental attitudes were (and would become even more) distinctive. The "southern complex that made the North into an evil genius continued to grow," writes Robert A. Rutland (*The Ordeal of the Constitution,* 1966), "until, seventy years later, it had worked itself into a militant obsession." Yet, in 1789, the American people as a whole had more in common culturally than the Spanish, French, or British. The economic sections of the United States might indeed quarrel; or they might, with wise leadership, learn to cooperate and complement one another.

Good fortune smiled upon the United States in 1789 in another respect—in acquiring the service of George Washington as its first president. Historians have never agreed about either the personality or the accomplishments of Washington. His image is so enshrined in the American imagination—a process of veneration which began long before his death—that even today it is difficult to separate the man and the myth. Marcus Cunliffe has suggested (*George Washington: Man and Monument,* 1958) that not only does the myth obscure the man but that "his personality baffles because it presents the mystery of no mystery." Was Washington simply a mediocre individual, a man of no outstanding talents? Several contemporaries thought so. As early as 1777 John Adams rather egotistically confided that "altho I honour him for his good qualities, yet in this house [the Continental Congress] I feel myself his Superior." No one has ever claimed that Washington was an original thinker. Nor was he a crusader, or brilliant intellectual, or daring reformer, or administrative genius. Still his other qualities—his dedicated patriotism, his unassailable character, his inexhaustible patience and determination to build a free and strong America— have seemed too perfect for any mere mortal. Yet, in the words of Dumas Malone, commenting on Douglas S. Freeman's multi-volume study of Washington (*George Washington: A Biography,* 1948-1957): "The verdict of the scrupulous historian after years of unremitting inquiry is that, as nearly as can be in human life, the legend and the man were identical."

As president, Washington followed the same pattern of behavior that characterized his leadership of the revolutionary armies. He was not inventive, and rarely did he initiate; rather he depended upon the advice of others. Some historians have suggested that Alexander Hamilton all but dominated the first executive. "Slow of mind," Alexander De Conde has written (*Entangling Alliance: Politics and Diplomacy under George Washington*, 1958), "he took his ideas and theories, without much question, from Hamilton." But Washington never tried in any way to evade the responsibility of making decisions. If on many occasions he sided with Hamilton rather than Jefferson or Madison, credit is largely due to the persuasive abilities of America's first secretary of the treasury. After all, Washington had much more in common with his fellow Virginians: a mutual love of the land and the plantation way of life which Hamilton could never share or even appreciate. To overcome this natural bias and to agree with Hamilton's economic proposals, which many Virginians deprecated, is also a tribute to Washington's objectivity and independence.

As Commander-in-Chief during the Revolution, Washington acted with an instinctive caution, weighing the consequences of each movement. In the pithy summation of his biographer, Douglas S. Freeman, Washington sought "the most gain for the least gore." Likewise, as president, he never acted precipitately. Conscious that every gesture could set a style, and every action an executive precedent, his political behavior was carefully calculated to abide by the spirit of the Constitution. Personally he indulged himself in the accoutrements of aristocracy—a handsome coach and livery, and powdered lackeys— for Washington believed it important to maintain a dignity befitting the office of president. A thin line sometimes seemed to separate the high-toned social etiquette from developing into outright monarchical practices. But that line was precisely Washington's unimpeachable virtue and his devotion to republicanism.

In 1797, Washington stepped down after eight turbulent

years. Much of the nation's history for that period—foreign affairs, economic legislation, religious practices, civil liberties, western development, constitutional law—reflected the dispute between Federalists and Republicans. Partisan battles of unparalleled ferocity, but kept within the framework of the Constitution, divided Americans into two political camps. Washington did not escape from these battles unscathed. His philosophy was to keep aloof from political warfare (he hated factionalism and was alarmed by the growth of parties) but more and more he could not escape identification with the Federalists. Republican newspapers came to question his judgments, vilify his character, and ultimately to declare him a traitor whose reputation gave a "currency to political iniquity and to legalized corruption." In 1797 Washington returned to the quiet of Mount Vernon with unfeigned relief, and with the satisfying knowledge of purpose well accomplished.

Historian John A. Carroll has listed no fewer than ten achievements of Washington's two administrations. During his presidency the United States government:

1. "gained its executive and legislative precedents,
2. appended a bill of rights to the Constitution,
3. established its credit at home and abroad,
4. fostered manufacturing and encouraged commerce,
5. survived a serious insurrection in the mountains of Pennsylvania,
6. secured the transmontane frontier against Indian depredations,
7. effected the removal of British troops from the Old Northwest,
8. checked Spanish encroachments in the Old Southwest and obtained transit rights on the Mississippi,
9. forged a policy for the disposition of public lands, and
10. avoided involvement in the vortex of European wars."

These achievements, it should be emphasized, were accomplished under Washington's guidance but not necessarily by him. Equal credit belongs to particular members of Congress and the diplomatic corps, and especially to the cabinet that developed during this era. Yet in a sense Washington left unresolved as many problems as were solved, and one might argue that he helped to create a few new ones. The proclamation of neutrality and Jay's treaty may have satisfied the British (a later generation would use the ugly word "appeased") but these actions aggravated American relations with France. The suppression of the Whiskey Rebellion served to spur the growth of party spirit which Washington abhorred. "The President is fortunate to get off just as the bubble is bursting," Jefferson predicted in 1797, "leaving others to hold the bag."

Washington is regarded by scholars as America's second greatest president (after Lincoln) not only, or even mainly, because of the positive accomplishments of his administration, but also for other reasons. In any government where traditional authority has been overthrown, states Seymour Lipset, a new basis of political loyalty ("legitimacy") can best be established through popular veneration of a national hero ("charismatic authority"). Thomas Jefferson put the matter in simpler terms when he noted in 1790: "If the President can be preserved a few years till habits of authority and obedience can be established generally, we have nothing to fear." Unlike so many other revolutionary heroes throughout history, Washington rejected the possibility of turning the presidency into a constitutional monarchy or military regime. And, by agreeing to serve not one, but two terms of office, Washington gave the new nation what above all else it needed: time.

The Constitution committed the nation to republicanism, outlined the mechanics of representation, sketched the form of the national government, and added (belatedly in the Bill of Rights) certain guarantees of individual liberties. Beyond this, however, the Constitution offered no specific solutions to national problems—for example, slavery or the payment of the national debts. Rather, it was meant to be a vehicle by means of which each generation could seek answers to contemporary problems within the context of the document. But even the context was not always clear. "Most of the articles in this system, which convey powers of any considerable importance are conceived in general and indefinite terms," commented a brilliant Antifederalist under the pen name Brutus, "which are either equivocal, ambiguous, or which require long definitions to unfold the extent of their meaning." This ambiguity of the Constitution has been its greatest asset, but sometimes its weakness. Could Congress incorporate a national bank or appropriate money to aid business? Was the carriage tax constitutional? Did the President, without the consent of Congress, have the right to declare American neutrality in 1793? Was the Sedition Act within the letter of the Constitution? In each case the Federalist party answered affirmatively; the Republicans, negatively. Both parties accepted the Constitution, the French traveler Rochefoucault-Liancourt observed, but each group learned how to use the document for its own designs.

The design of the Federalist party seemed clear enough: to strengthen the national government. Only then would property be secure, freedom assured, and independence guaranteed. To accomplish this it was imperative that the Constitution be broadly construed in all its parts. Republicans feared this doctrine, for they believed it would lead inevitably to a Leviathan state of unrestricted powers. They viewed government in the fashion of eighteenth century anti-monarchists, as a necessary evil, to be expressly limited, constantly patrolled, and periodically reviewed. Federalists, particularly Alexander Hamilton, viewed government in modern terms, as a positive and expanding force for economic growth. Republicans believed in the efficacy of state government as a safer repository of all residual powers unnecessary for national purposes. Federalists regarded the doctrine of states' rights as inherently divisive, the creed of self-interested, local politicos.

Perhaps the most important early conflict over constitutional interpretation was Thomas Jefferson's attempt in 1791 to persuade President Washington to veto the bill incorporating a Bank of the United States. "To take a single step beyond the boundaries . . . specially drawn around the powers of Congress," he prophesied, "is to take possession of a boundless field of power, no longer susceptible of any definition." Hamilton's rebuttal deserves its reputation as one of his ablest state papers: obviously, the authority to enact a bank was not specifically delegated to the national government; but it does not follow, therefore, that the act is unconstitutional. "The means by which national exigencies are to be provided for, national inconveniencies obviated, national prosperity promoted," Hamilton stated, "are of such infinite variety, extent, and complexity, that there must of necessity be great latitude of discretion in the selection and application of those means." The bank was one such means to achieve certain ends undoubtedly within the scope and purpose of the national government. "If the *end* be clearly comprehended within any of the specified powers," Hamilton reasoned, "and if the measure have an obvious relation to that *end,* and is not forbidden by any particular provision of the constitution, it may safely be deemed to come within the compass of the national authority."

Thus, almost from its inception, and despite the fact that many members of the Constitutional Convention sat in the first Congress, the vagueness of the Constitution caused partisan wrangling over the core problem of federalism: the division of powers. The celebrated ambiguity of the Constitution has allowed a document written for an agricultural country of four million people huddled in thirteen states along the Atlantic seacoast to serve a nation through unprecedented growth and metamorphosis into an urbanized and industrialized world power.

But the penalty has been to subject each generation of Americans to a reargument of its meaning, much along the lines which separated the Federalists and Republicans.

Jefferson and Hamilton realized that mankind was blended of good and evil, and that American character especially seemed composed of equalitarian impulse balanced by economic self-interest. But whereas Jefferson recognized the corrupt elements in man's nature, he had little doubt that reason would ultimately triumph over passion. "Nature has implanted in our breasts," wrote Jefferson, "a love of others, a sense of duty to them, a moral instinct." The intelligent politician "who would do his country the most good . . . must go quietly with the prejudices of the majority until he can lead them into reason." Hamilton, on the other hand, was convinced that the baser instincts of mankind were dominant and immutable. A wise governor must accept the "depravity of human nature" as a fact, utilize it, manipulate it, and turn it to the national advantage. Jefferson's faith that mankind could be improved through the influence of liberal education and the beneficent effects of free government was scorned by Hamilton as a "deceitful dream of a Golden Age." Because Jefferson had a greater trust in mankind, he believed that a free choice by an informed electorate must normally result in the election of a talented and intelligent "natural aristocracy." Hamilton could not agree. He intended to equate economic wealth with political wisdom. He distrusted the people, particularly when they acted *en masse*. "The people are turbulent and changing," was Hamilton's dictum, "they seldom judge or determine right."

Federalists and Republicans were constant in their vigilance against any form of tyranny. But Republicans believed the greater possibility of tyranny or oligarchy were contained within the presidential and senatorial offices, and they particularly resisted any augmentations of executive power. The Republican nightmare was an elected king, with all the trappings of European courts, a monarch infinitely worse, many believed, than an hereditary one. Federalists, on the other hand, panicked at the thought of a tyrannous majority. Their nightmare was a mob looting warehouses, burning mortgages, invading courthouses, intimidating gentlemen; or their national representatives passing paper-money laws and moratoriums.

Federalists envisioned a day when America would become a great power in the world, respected by and at peace with all nations. "Unshackle your minds," Noah Webster advised his countrymen in 1790. "You have an empire to raise and support by your exertions." To achieve this goal it was necessary to cultivate steady habits at home and to cease local jealousies. The American character was then in the process of jelling, and once fixed would be difficult to alter. Economic stability was imperative. Taxes must be raised and debts paid, so that credit at home and abroad could be restored and the American financial structure set for all time on a firm foundation. The Republicans did not disagree. Their dream was somewhat different, more oriented towards the West, but like the Federalists they wanted American credit established and American prestige enhanced.

Federalists were painfully frank in their belief that a simple and undiluted democracy was the worst form of government. They regarded property as sacrosanct, and the rich and wellborn, sober men of the business community as specially endowed with those virtues which fitted them for rule. America to them was a corporation, but they and not the stockholders were the directors of its destiny. In the balance, the means Federalists employed to maintain order were questionable and probably unnecessary. But their substantial contributions to the creation of the American nation are indisputable. Before the eighteenth century passed American leaders had organized a government, strengthened it against external enemies, nursed it through internal dissensions, purged it of inherited debts, restored its national credit, quieted its revolutionary impulses, and assured its future prosperity. These were no mean accomplishments, for in essence problems were solved which had bedeviled the British administration of the colonies and caused the downfall of the Articles of Confederation.

What was the Republican role during these first twelve years of the Constitution? Was the minority party contribution essentially a negative one? What concretely and positively did Republicans add to the national foundation? All too often they are seen as natural law philosophers, theoreticians inclined toward an archaic and static agrarianism. The Federalists, Henry Stimson wrote to Theodore Roosevelt in 1910, were "the doers" and the nation needed business-minded pragmatists rather than fuzzy-minded idealists. After Jefferson assumed the presidency, and because he was faced for the first time with the prosaic problems of having to run the country, many historians deem his administration a success only because he "outfederalized the federalists." This interpretation is not correct.

In sum, many factors operated in favor of the development of an effective federal system, national unity, and democratic growth. Auspicious conditions at the outset of the Constitution aided in its favorable reception. Washington's leadership for eight years was indispensable. But above all other significant causes, the accomplishments of the Federalist era resulted from a perverse and curious partnership. More explicitly, they resulted not despite, but because of, the conflict between emerging parties. Referring to the antagonism between Jefferson and Hamilton, Broadus Mitchell has noted (*Alexander Hamilton,* 1957-62): "Their fierce espousal of rival principles or policies issued, as neither could foresee, in complementary achievement." Like the rubbing of two sticks, Federalist and Republican generated much smoke, and some heat, but they also breathed the fire of life into the American experiment.

PUBLIC CREDIT
AND MAJORITY RULE

The figure of Alexander Hamilton evokes the fiercest passions of American historians. He has been alternately praised and condemned as a selfless nationalist or scheming monarchist, a financial wizard or meretricious demagogue, a dedicated patriot or Machiavellian intriguer. Hamilton's critics have chosen to emphasize some undeniable inconsistencies between his words and his actions. Joseph Charles, for example (*The Origins of the American Party System,* 1956), refers to Hamilton's virtual promise in *The Federalist* that no excise taxes would be enacted if the Constitution were ratified; yet excise taxes were an integral part of his financial program. Charles quotes from a speech of Hamilton at the New York ratifying convention in which he extolled the "great source of free government, popular election, [which] should be perfectly pure"; and mentions Hamilton's attempt in 1800 to void the popular vote of New York City which had resulted in the election of a Republican majority. Again, Charles notes Hamilton's expressed desire, in *The Federalist,* to erect "one great American system, superior to the control of all transatlantic force or influence"; and compares this statement with Hamilton's pro-British sympathies during his tenure as Secretary of the Treasury. Hamilton went so far in these sympathies, according to recent documentation by Julian Boyd (*Number 7: Alexander Hamilton's Secret Attempts to Control American Foreign Policy,* 1964), that he was known to British agents and his information of cabinet meetings was forwarded to England under the cipher key of "No. 7."

In judging such behavior, pro-Hamilton scholars have listed some extenuating factors. Hamilton's inconsistencies were no worse than those of Madison, Jefferson, or any other political leader facing a clash between ideals and realities. Further, Hamilton regarded his position as one of *primus inter pares,* and therefore entitled to have a voice in foreign policy. Finally, reprehensible as Hamilton's behavior may have been, was it or was it not in the national interest? Joseph Charles as well as many other historians affirm that Hamilton's systematic fabrications were opposed to the national interest. His defenders maintain that Hamilton's actions may have been indiscreet, even unwise, but these very acts were the result of his zealous Americanism, and his single-minded desire to save his economic program. Without Hamilton's program, the United States might have been swamped by unpaid debts, bankruptcies, and general chaos.

In October, 1789, Congress requested Hamilton, as Secretary of the Treasury, to prepare a Report on Public Credit. Within three months, after a painstaking collection of relevant fiscal data and a canvassing of opinions, Hamilton submitted his plan. The Report anticipated many opposition arguments, but failed to convince those who saw in it dangerous precedents for America. Everyone agreed that the foreign debt must be honorably retired, but Hamilton's report contained audacious proposals which went far beyond mere recommendations for payment.

First, the Report suggested that the entire debt be paid at face value, with no distinction made between the original purchaser and the current holder of the debt.

James Madison, Hamilton's old ally and co-author of *The Federalist,* at this time a Representative from Virginia, delivered the most reasoned objections, on moral grounds, to the projected method for paying the domestic part of the debt. Many patriots, said Madison, who had helped America during the desperate days of the Revolution, were forced by economic necessity in the depression years of the 1780's to sell their securities at a fraction of their face value. Madison was careful not to label current holders of the securities, as did some other congressmen, as "unconscionable speculators." But he did feel it "radically immoral and consequently impolitic" to shift the entire payment from the "gallant Earners of them to that class of people who now take their places." Madison believed "present holders . . . [should] have the highest price [for their securities] which has prevailed in the market." The difference in money between face value and market value would be given to the original purchaser. Thus, the current holder would have a profit, and the original purchaser would receive the residue. "This will not do perfect justice," said Madison, "but it will do more real justice, and perform more of the public faith, than any other expedient proposed."

Hamilton rejected Madison's proposition as unjust and impractical. The current holder, he felt, was entitled to every cent. "The established rules of morality and justice," said Hamilton, answering Madison in kind, "are applicable to nations as well as to individuals. . . . A relaxation of this kind would tend to dissolve all social obligations—to render all rights precarious and to introduce a general dissoluteness and corruption of morals." Since twenty-nine of the sixty-four members of the lower House were security holders, Hamilton's argument carried much weight and Madison's proposal was defeated by a vote of 36 to 13. An angry poet commented "On the rejection of Mr. Madison's motion":

> A soldier's pay are rags and fame,
> A wooden leg—a deathless name.
> To specs, both *in* and *out* of Cong,
> The four and six per cents belong!

It is instructive to pause a moment to examine how two modern scholars handle the clash between Hamilton and Madison. Broadus Mitchell, biographer of Hamilton, reminds the reader that Madison in 1783 "promised that [the] U.S. would honor the domestic debt by whomever held." Irving Brant, biographer of Madison (*James Madison,* 1948-61), argues that circumstances were quite different by 1790 (there had been heavy speculation in these securities) and the change fully justified Madison's revised views. Mitchell rather coyly suggests that Madison's sudden change of attitude about Hamilton's policies was inexplicable unless possibly some unknown evil influence persuaded him to such a course. "Jefferson arrived on the scene just at this time," writes Mitchell. "As it was not he, but Madison, who conspicuously reversed himself from nationalist to sectionalist, was Jefferson the alembic?" Brant, always careful to reject any implication that Jefferson was mentor of the two, makes it quite plain that Madison acted for himself. Madison, says Brant, "deliberately abandoned his majority leadership when he saw that the price of keeping it was to become the tool of financial oligarchy." Mitchell has emphasized, as did Hamilton, the impracticability of Madison's proposals. (Joseph Charles maintains that they were completely feasible.) Brant has emphasized, as did Madison, the injustice of Hamilton's proposals. Madison's plan was defeated, according to Mitchell, because he "did not know the terrain as Hamilton did." Madison's plan was defeated, according to Brant, because "the justice he called for would hurt the rich, help the poor, and save nothing to the taxpayer."

The difference of opinion between Hamilton and Madison is significant because from it can be traced the split in the original ranks of Federalism. Hamilton's position was based on both legality and expediency, the defense of property rights, the necessity of establishing an early precedent that would give confidence to capitalists, and a profound appreciation of the creative function of the speculator. The higher virtue, to Hamilton, was not abstract equity but current necessity. Madison's position was based on his sympathetic concern for the original purchasers, a morality which was outraged by the effect of Hamilton's policy, which would enrich the venal speculators he despised. The higher virtue, to Madison, was a humanitarian concern for the common man. (Here was the genesis of the Republican party.) The distinction in views is so crucial that most later scholars, particularly biographers, cannot seem to avoid reflecting and thus defending the arguments of their subjects.

Second, Hamilton's Report provided that the national government assume the responsibility of paying all Revolutionary War debts *of the states* as of 1790.

The division in Congress on this issue was acrimonious, and depended entirely upon whether or not the representatives spoke for the people of a state with little or large indebtedness. For example, congressmen from Massachusetts, New York, and South Carolina, each of which had been delinquent in meeting its obligations, favored Hamilton's system. Georgia, Maryland, and North Carolina, each of which had expended considerably less during the Revolution, and consequently had smaller unpaid debts, were opposed to the measure. The case of Virginia was unique. By distributing land warrants, and by using depreciated currency, Virginia had succeeded in reducing its debt by some forty per cent. Hamilton's plan would effectively penalize Virginians by obligating them to help pay the debts of other—mainly Northern—states. Moreover, assumption would double the size of the national debt. Who would bear the burden? And who would benefit? The Virginia legislature passed a remonstrance against assumption, drafted by Patrick Henry, which intoned: "In an agricultural country like this, therefore, to erect, and concentrate, and perpetuate a large monied interest, is a measure which your memorialists apprehend, must in the course of human events produce one or other of two evils, the prostration of agriculture at the feet of commerce, or a change in the present form of federal government, fatal to the existence of American liberty."

While tempers flared, and the first signs of sectionalism

appeared, James Madison once more sought a compromise that would be acceptable to all parties. The concept of assumption was not wrong, but it should have been based on state indebtedness as of 1783, when the peace treaty with England was signed, rather than 1790. Hamilton again disagreed, but some modifications were arranged to make assumption more palatable to the Virginians. Even then, the act did not pass until Jefferson and Madison won from Hamilton the promise to use his influence, particularly with Robert Morris, to have the national capital moved permanently to the Potomac after a ten year residence in Philadelphia. In exchange, the two Virginians agreed to reverse the votes of enough Southerners to guarantee passage of the assumption bill in its second test. It was a bargain Jefferson always regretted. "Of all the errors of my political life," he wrote to Washington in 1792, "this has occasioned me the deepest regret."

Third, Hamilton proposed that the combined national and state domestic debts, both principal and interest, which he estimated at $79,000,000, be funded—that is to say, the national government would issue negotiable bonds (there were six options) to holders of the debt. A percentage of the revenue would be earmarked to guarantee payment on these bonds at stipulated periods.

Here was the core of the Hamiltonian scheme. At one stroke comparatively worthless certificates of indebtedness were transformed into fluid capital which would stimulate the economy. Hamilton spelled this out in his Report. "Trade is extended by it, because there is a larger capital to carry it on, and the merchant can at the same time, afford to trade for smaller profits; as his stock which, when unemployed, brings him in an interest from the Government, serves him also as money when he has a call for it in his commercial operations." The "new capital stock," reported the *Gazette of the United States* in 1792, ". . . is directed into every branch of business, giving life and vigor to industry in its infinitely diversified operations." Further, since the debt would be held by the wealthier citizens, it would be to their obvious advantage to support the new Constitution and national government. The debt would be the binding force of the union.

Opponents condemned the speculative frenzy which developed with the first introduction of Hamilton's Report. They knew that many congressmen were hastily buying securities. They realized, moreover, that funding and assumption would lessen the taxing ability of the states as it increased that of the national government. To that extent state authority would be curtailed and national authority enhanced. These taxes would flow from poor to rich, from South to North, from yeoman to speculator. In short, they believed that Hamilton's program inflated the debt needlessly and without justice, under the specious doctrine (which Hamilton specifically disclaimed) that a public debt was somehow a blessing.

Fourth, a second report which Hamilton submitted at the end of 1790 recommended the establishment of a public national bank to be incorporated by an act of Congress, in which the government of the United States would be a minority stockholder.

Hamilton believed the Bank of the United States would be useful as a depository of government funds, and act as a collecting and disbursing agent of the Treasury. It would be required, when requested, to make loans to the federal government. It would provide the country with a sound and extensive currency. (At the time only three commercial banks were in operation—in Philadelphia, New York and Boston.) It would, like funding and assumption, increase the fluid capital essential for economic growth. Neither Hamilton nor anyone else could foresee still another of its functions. As the number of banks increased—by 1800 there were 29; by 1811, 90—the national bank, writes Bray Hammond (*Banks and Politics in*

America, 1957), "automatically exercised a general restraint upon the banking system." But in 1790 the political significance of the Bank probably equalled its economic importance. Since Bank stock could be subscribed by using a high proportion of the recently funded government bonds, the most influential class in America, the stockholders, would be even more committed by self-interest to support the federal government.

At this time Madison, not Jefferson, was regarded as the principal adversary of Hamilton's program. Modern scholars agree that Madison, more than any other person, was responsible for organizing the opposition. "Madison in truth was the great man of the party," writes Noble E. Cunningham *(The Jeffersonian Republicans: The Formation of Party Organization,* 1957), "and it was only natural that the Republican interest was often referred to as Madison's party." John C. Miller concurs *(The Federalist Era,* 1960) and adds: "If the reward had gone to the man who had done most for the Republican party, James Madison would have been its first candidate for the Presidency." In fact, Jefferson had not yet arrived in the capital (New York) when Madison commenced his opposition to the funding and assumption measures. Without a doubt Jefferson agreed with Madison's position, but as Secretary of State he was reluctant to interfere in the conflict. He had played no role in rousing popular opinion. Jefferson's public disagreement with Hamilton began with the issue of the Bank. It marked the first time that Republican opposition to a Hamiltonian measure was unqualified and uncompromising.

The supposed advantages of a national Bank were spurious, Republicans claimed. During times of prosperity the federal government could borrow money anywhere; in adversity the Bank would be reluctant to proffer loans. To make the Bank a depository and agent of federal funds, upon which it might issue currency or make loans, was to endow it with monopolistic powers which would succeed ultimately in destroying all other financial competition. The same small moneyed class which owned the federal debt would more or less be the stockholders of the Bank, and would reap its profits from the labor of the American yeoman. Farmers would suffer since the Bank would favor business interests. The Bank would be an "engine of influence," capable of polluting every operation of government. "Who are most to be dreaded," John Taylor asked in a pamphlet attacking the Bank, "the *nominal* or *real* lords of America? It is evident that exorbitant wealth constitutes the substance and danger of aristocracy. Money in a state of civilization is power . . ."

Fifth, in order to obtain money to pay the interest and principal of the combined debt, Hamilton urged and Congress in 1791 enacted an excise tax on distilled whiskey.

Most federal income was derived from the tariff. Raising the tariff to provide more revenue would simply encourage smuggling. Too, a tariff was uncertain, Hamilton argued, easily disrupted by wars and blockades. A more dependable supplement was required. From previous experience Hamilton was well aware that an excise tax on whiskey would be decidedly unpopular. However, he claimed it would be more equitable to shift part of the tax burden from Eastern merchants to Western farmers. If Americans regarded the excise on whiskey as an intolerable burden, let them consume less. Some critics believe that Hamilton would have welcomed an opportunity to display the enforcement authority of the central government.

Several Republicans, including James Madison, voted for the excise because they thought it imperative as a source of revenue. But Southerners in general opposed it. Congressman James Jackson of Georgia argued that his constituents "have been long in the habit of getting drunk and they will get drunk in defiance of . . . all the excise duties Congress might be weak or wicked enough to impose." In Western Pennsylvania, because it was easier and more economical to transport a barrel of whiskey than a bushel of grain, alcohol was used as money, or for barter, or shipped across the Alleghenies to be sold in Eastern markets. These farmers regarded the excise, which amounted to twenty-five per cent of the net price of the whiskey, as unreasonably high. At first stills of under fifty gallons capacity were exempt, but after 1792 even this exemption was removed. Moreover, those accused of violating the law had to travel great distances to appear before a federal court.

The entire Hamiltonian system, according to Republicans, subverted the purpose, the letter, and the spirit of the Constitution. And why had Hamilton and his followers established this program? For personal power? Yes. To strengthen the national government? Definitely. But their ultimate goal, well hidden from the people, Jefferson and Madison believed, was the creation of a monarchy in America.

The warfare continues in the pages of the history books. Like the contemporaries involved in this struggle, so scholars have created an historical no-man's-land over Hamilton's policies. Fifty years ago it became the fashion, set by Charles Beard, to recognize the marriage of commercial and other monetary interests to national power, sanctified by the Constitution, and consummated by Hamilton's fiscal program. In a volume of epochal influence (*An Economic Interpretation of the Constitution*, 1913), Beard maintained that the Constitution was the work of particular capitalistic classes who staged a conservative counterrevolution against the radical agrarians. And in a notable sequel (*Economic Origins of Jeffersonian Democracy*, 1915), Beard insisted that Hamilton's program was the logical payoff to these propertied classes for their continued allegiance to the new central government. Hamilton knew, wrote Beard, "that the government could not stand if its sole basis was the platonic support of genial well-wishers. He knew that it had been created in response to interested demands and not out of any fine-spun theories of political science. Therein he displayed the penetrating wisdom which placed him among the great statesmen of all time."

The Federalist party, Beard attempted to prove, derived from those who had advocated adoption of the Constitution. Hamilton's support was centered mainly in cities and in regions where commercial or financial or manufacturing interests were dominant. The Republican party, on the other hand, derived from those who had been Antifederalist opponents of ratification. Their support was centered mainly in rural areas, but led by Southern slave-holding aristocrats. To put the matter in one phrase, the struggle over the Constitution and the subsequent political warfare between Federalist and Republican was fundamentally economic in nature, a battle between agrarians and capitalists for control of America.

Virtually every part of the Beardian thesis has been vigorously challenged (and, with qualifications, fiercely defended):

1. Recent works have seriously questioned Beard's evidence and thus his conclusions on the writing and ratification of the Constitution. (See, for example, Robert E. Brown, *Charles Beard and the Constitution,* 1956; and Forrest McDonald's *We the People,* 1963, and *E Pluribus Unum,* 1965). One might argue that if the critics are correct, if the foundation of Beard's interpretation is wrong, then what follows from it for the 1790's must be considered as highly suspect.

2. Many scholars reject what they regard as an oversimplified view of the sweep of American development as a conflict of opposites: North v. South, urban v. rural, industrial v. agrarian, capitalist v. debtor. Historical writing inevitably reflects its time of composition. Beard and his contemporaries were influenced by the clear-cut polarities of the Populist and Progressive eras; mid-twentieth century scholars echo the endless complexities of their own age. Thus, polarities are admitted to exist, but exceptions to them are numerous, and the student is warned against attractive but sometimes specious historical

formulae. "Republicanism versus Federalism . . . [is] by no means clear cut," writes Marcus Cunliffe (*The Nation Takes Shape,* 1959). "It is not just that we are uncertain which side is hero and which villain, but that we are not always able to say with confidence which side is which, so confusing and sudden are the shifts in allegiance."

3. Numerous studies have tested the Beardian thesis on the sources of Federalist and Republican support by research into specific areas and classes. One would suppose that so much historiographical activity would solve the problem of whether or not Beard was right. But at best the results are unclear and even contradictory. Harry M. Tinckom (*The Republicans and Federalists in Pennsylvania,* 1950) concludes that in Pennsylvania the Antifederalist opponents of the Constitution formed the nucleus of the Republican party. Harry Ammon, on the other hand, in an essay on Republican party formation in Virginia (which appeared in *The Journal of Southern History,* 1953) finds "no significant connection between the anti-federalists of 1788 and the Republicans, nor between the federalists and the subsequent Federalist party."

4. Some scholars who admire Hamilton, such as Broadus Mitchell, feel that Beard's frank opinion that the Secretary of the Treasury appealed to an economic elite is much too extremely stated. Other scholars, such as Joseph Charles, have utilized Beard's evidence not to praise but rather to condemn Hamilton. Thus Beard is doubly rejected: by those who say his appreciation of Hamilton is untrustworthy, and by those pro-Jeffersonian writers who believe that his conclusions are incorrect.

Usually scholars hostile to Hamilton at least acknowledge the wisdom of his financial policies. An exception to this rule has been Joseph Charles. Like Jefferson and Madison, Charles believes that Hamilton's program was unnecessary and intended to subvert "the type of government which most well-informed men thought they were supporting when they voted to accept the Constitution." So hostile is Charles' study, according to John C. Miller, "that it reads like a political tract of the 1790's." However, most scholars still would agree that Hamilton's intention, simply stated, was to build a strong and efficient central government, the cornerstone of which would be a restored public credit, fluid capital, increased land values, sound currency, and governmental promotion and protection of industry. Most scholars would also agree that Republican fears that Hamiltonian Federalists desired a monarchy patterned after the British were unfounded (as were Federalist beliefs that Republicans would institute a reign of terror patterned after the French). It is obvious that Jeffersonian Republicans, very much like Jacksonian Democrats of a later period, showed no appreciation of the invaluable role of the national Bank in early American economic growth. American industrial development has vindicated Hamilton as the better prophet. Later Supreme Court decisions have, more often than not, corroborated the Hamiltonian interpretation of the Constitution, not the Jeffersonian.

Of prime importance to these pages, however, are the contemporary images held by the Republicans. The crucial fact is that the Republicans saw Hamilton as a scheming minister operating under President Washington's imprimatur. They were convinced that certain Federalists aimed at monarchy; and that this goal had been their secret design for many years. Were not Hamilton's constitutional doctrines roughly equivalent in effect to Parliament's Declaratory Act? Were there not some obvious parallels between the Virginia Stamp Act resolution and Virginia's protest against assumption? Hamilton must have thought so, for he remarked: "This is the first symptom of a spirit which must either be killed or will kill the Constitution of the United States." Was not Hamilton's pernicious influence felt in President Washington's denunciation of the Democratic societies? "An extraordinary act of boldness," wrote Jefferson in disgust, "of which we have seen so many from the faction of monocrats." Twenty years before, citizens protesting unjust taxation were called Sons of Liberty and their occasional acts of intimidation were applauded. Now they were referred to as "armed banditti" by the President, who, in 1794, dispatched 12,600 militia to Western Pennsylvania to suppress the Whiskey Rebellion. Neither Jefferson nor Madison approved of the uprising, but they considered the display of military power by the national government as totally unwarranted. Only twenty ragtag prisoners were taken. "An insurrection was announced and proclaimed and armed against," said Jefferson sardonically, "but could never be found."

These were revolutionary conditions, and Republican leaders were indeed conscious of the possibilities of disunion. They could have destroyed the Constitution. By their lights they had every reason to do so. Given the inflammable temper of America during Washington's administrations, one well-placed match might have ignited an insurrectionary blaze which would have gutted the central government. But Madison and Jefferson cautioned their followers that they must neither rebel nor secede. Even under the next administration of John Adams, and despite greater provocations, Republican leaders continued to follow a course which under the circumstances can only be described as conservative, pragmatic, and democratic. For America the age of blood had passed, replaced by that of ink. Revolutionary tactics were unnecessary when disagreements could be peacefully settled within the confines of the Constitution. The political convention was substituted for revolutionary barricades. Their followers, Madison and Jefferson believed, could and should incite public opinion, but they must abide by a majority rule fairly obtained and constitutionally practiced. It was a lesson that penetrated to the core of the American character.

The work of Jefferson and Madison should be considered

in the nature of a great collaboration. In opposition to the Federalists, and in the later years of Republican rule, they cooperated in a spirit of trust and confidence. What Madison started, Jefferson continued, and Federalists came to believe the former was acting as a stalking horse for the latter's presidential intentions. They labeled Madison "General" and Jefferson "Generalissimo." Certainly Madison performed the initial hard work of party organization and direction, but Jefferson, with Madison's complete approbation, emerged to become both the titular and real head of the Republican structure.

Much has been written about the gap that often existed between Jefferson's opinions and actions. But that gap can be explained in the 1790's in part by the fact that Jefferson was constantly attempting to redress the effects of Hamiltonian measures. Jefferson was no doctrinaire radical who followed theory to the bitter end regardless of the consequences. His quest was for a democratic state; the problem, how to achieve it. In 1776 the American revolution was a last resort to Jefferson, peaceful means having been exhausted. But in the 1790's, despite many provocations, his commitment was to legal, not illegal political action. He was convinced that the majority of the American people were republican in spirit and, when sufficiently alerted to the dangers, would vote Republican in practice. He believed that if the Hamiltonians could buy the loyalty of propertied aristocrats to support an all-powerful central government, Republicans could operate on the reason of the masses to support a more equitable and democratic federal division. The Constitution itself was not at fault. All that was required, he told Madison in 1797, "was to put our vessel on her republican tack before she should be thrown too much to leeward of her true principles."

After his election in 1801, Jefferson was gratified to reflect that for an infant nation the Americans had exhibited a surprising maturity in their acceptance of majority rule. Surely this contribution was as significant for American democracy as Hamilton's was for the economic well-being of the early republic.

LIMITS OF THE AMERICAN
POLITICAL TRADITION

According to his grandson, Thomas Jefferson never considered Federalist fulminations "as abusing him; they had never known him. They had created an imaginary being clothed with odious attributes, to whom they gave his name; and it was against that creature of their imaginations they had levelled their anathemas." After the political passions of the 1790's had long settled, John Adams reminisced in a letter to Jefferson: "Both parties have excited artificial terrors and if I were summoned as a witness to say upon oath, which party had excited . . . the most terror, and which had really felt the most, I could not give a more sincere answer, than in the vulgar style 'Put them in a bag and shake them, and then see which comes out first.' "

During the administration of John Adams, and culminating in the presidential election of 1800, the American people exhibited a fiery partisanship rarely equalled in subsequent years. Vitriolic newspaper articles and pamphlets, and passionate debates in Congress resulted in massive political distrust and misunderstanding. Normal differences between Federalists and Republicans widened and were exaggerated into monstrous symbols. The fears and terrors each party felt may have been "artificial" in retrospect, but at the time they seemed real enough. "To crush democracy by force was the ultimate recourse of Hamilton," wrote Henry Adams in 1879. "To crush that force was the determined intention of Jefferson." Is this correct? How accurately did contemporary representations reflect the true aims and motivations of each party? How close did America come to disunion?

Without a doubt Federalist conservatism was curdling into authoritarianism. As Republican party strength increased, Federalist politicians arrogated to themselves sole custodianship of the Constitution. They claimed to be the loyal originators and ardent defenders of a document that Republicans had never really believed in and now wished to destroy. Convinced of the infallibility of their doctrines, the Federalists became increasingly intolerant of heretical opinions. This was natural enough. Similar pressures have attempted to eliminate democratic rights in many revolutionary movements in their early national stage. "To create a stable, representative, decision-making process that provides a legitimate place for opposition," writes Seymour Lipset, ". . . is extremely difficult in any polity. It is particularly problematic in new states which must be concerned also with the sheer problem of the survival of national authority itself." In the vocabulary of the twentieth century, the Federalists aimed at creating a single-party state. But precisely how far did Federalist leaders intend to carry their drift toward authoritarianism? Would they void elections if the results were contrary to their expectations? Would they use military force to punish disobedience? Would they rather destroy the union than see Jefferson President?

Republicans also, as a counter to Federalist alarmism, seemed to be moving toward an extreme. Madison's defense of the Constitution had provided his party with a philosophic base which rejected one of the major tenets of the Antifederalists of 1787. Given the huge territory of the United States, Antifederalists had argued, it would be impossible to maintain a republican form of government under the Constitution. The axiom derived from the Greeks and was supported by all political writers. But their favorite philosopher was Montesquieu, and over and over the Antifederalists had quoted—or misquoted—from his work, *The Spirit of the Laws*. They lauded the Swiss Helvetian confederation as a practical application of the theory that only in small areas could a government of the people survive. All history had shown that large areas required an emperor or military chief to control the people by force. When a small democratic state enlarged its boundaries (and Antifederalists invariably cited the case of the Italian Republic extending its dominions) inevitably the government became despotic.

Thus, the Constitution was a bold experiment, and no one knew this better than Madison, who had provided an answer to the Antifederalist followers of Montesquieu. All governments, large and small, said Madison, are prone to the machinations of selfish men and special interests. If freedom is better safeguarded in small areas, where government is not so far removed from the people, yet the sword of political logic cuts two ways. It is easier in small than in large areas for a faction to gain control and to rule tyrannically. And if freedom is threatened in a national government responsible for a great territorial area, where one man may develop monarchical powers, the same sword cuts in the opposite direction. For the central government will contain Northern, Southern, and Western interests; landed, mercantile, and a host of lesser interests; and it will be difficult—not impossible but improbable—for any one faction to seize and to maintain control. "In the extended republic of the United States and among the great variety of interests, parties and sects which it embraces," wrote Madison in *Federalist* No. 50, "a coalition of a majority of the whole society could seldom take place on any other principles than those of justice and the general good." The Constitution, therefore, by recognizing that mankind is in part dominated and directed by the passion for power, particularly economic power, turns evil into good by balancing these forces and requiring a national concensus on each issue. "I suspect that the doctrine that small states alone are fitted to be republics," Jefferson wrote in 1795 to Francois d'Ivernois, "will be exploded by experience. . . . Perhaps it will be found that to obtain a just republic . . . it must be so extensive that local egoisms may never reach its greater part. . . . The smaller the societies, the more violent and more convulsive their schisms."

Did the Republicans repudiate these doctrines during the crises of the Adams administration? To be sure, as a reaction to increased Federalist authoritarianism, Republican emphasis veered toward states' rights. Neither party philosophy nor philosophers remained immobile in the 1790's. But precisely how far did Madison and Jefferson intend to carry states' rights doctrine? Would they endorse secession if Federalists made a mockery of the Bill of Rights? Would they advocate armed rebellion if Federalists thwarted the majority will? Would they rather destroy the union than see it converted into a veiled monarchy?

Jefferson and John Adams, the second President, shared a political association and personal friendship which, while strained on several occasions, stretched back over two decades. The two men disagreed about the nature of government, but their common bond was based on mutual honesty and respect. Both desired to calm political passions; both shared a distaste for Hamilton. At the outset Jefferson thought that Adams was the strongest barrier America possessed to block any aspirations Hamilton might have had for the presidency. In the early months of 1797 Adams made overtures to Jefferson and for a moment it seemed as if a coalition government might develop. (Jefferson was Vice President, having received but three less electoral votes than Adams.) Hamilton certainly thought a conspiracy was forming between the two old allies. But Madison warned Jefferson to be cautious. Oliver Wolcott, Jr., threatened to resign as Secretary of the Treasury if a Republican were named Minister to France. Soon any hope of reconciliation between Adams and Jefferson was broken by their divergent positions on foreign affairs; and further shattered by the Alien and Sedition Acts of June-July, 1798.

Ironically enough, it was Adams, Jefferson's long-time friend, who helped to instigate the alien and sedition legislation. Like Washington, Adams was troubled by the presence of French agents peddling the ideas of their revolution, actively interfering in American elections, and propagandizing resistance to what they considered the administration's pro-British policy. The XYZ Affair in particular convinced the Federalists that Republican criticism of the government was disloyal and could no longer be tolerated. "He that is not for us," the Federalist *Gazette of the United States* declared, "is against us." Federalists saw in every new immigrant a dangerous revolutionary who invariably joined the Republican party. Harrison G. Otis, a Massachusetts Federalist, complained that he "did not wish to invite hordes of wild Irishmen, nor the turbulent and disorderly of all parts of the world, to come here with a view to disturb our tranquillity, after having succeeded in the overthrow of their own Governments." In modern terms, they regarded Republicans as ranging from pink to red in political coloration. Therefore Federalists felt they were fully justified in the principles which lay behind the Alien and Sedition Acts. They hoped to cripple the Republican party by silencing their newspapers and by removing the sources of their support. In so doing, they would save America.

Few Federalists believed the Alien and Sedition Acts to be harsh or extreme. Quite the contrary, Federalists contended that the acts were careful to maintain the legal rights of citizens. For example, the proposal was seriously made and seconded that citizenship should be restricted to the native-born. Since this might be construed as unconstitutional, another Federalist suggested a term of probationary residence for aliens requesting citizenship of such length as to make it virtually impossible for any but a few immigrants ever to qualify. The final Naturaliza-

tion Act was less rigorous. It simply raised the residence require-
ment from five to fourteen years. "This restriction on the en-
franchisement of immigrants," writes James M. Smith (*Freedom's Fetters,* 1956), "dealt the Democratic-Republican party
a heavy blow by robbing it of an important element of its support."

Federalist hatred of aliens was typified by the remark of
President Adams's nephew, William Smith Shaw: "The grand
cause of all our present difficulties may be traced . . . to so
many *hordes of Foreigners* imigrating [*sic*] to America. . . .
Let us no longer pray that America may become an asylum to
all nations." William Cobbett, ultra-Federalist editor of *Porcu-
pine's Gazette,* went further: "Were I president I would hang
them or they would murder me. I never would hold the sword
of justice, and suffer such miscreants to escape its edge." The
Act Concerning Aliens gave the president authority to deport
any alien he deemed a danger to the United States. Originally,
however, the bill provided for a possible sentence of life imprisonment at hard labor for any alien who, once deported, returned voluntarily to the United States. This was considered
rather severe and on the motion of Robert G. Harper the penalty
for this offense was changed to imprisonment, "so long as in
the opinion of the President the public safety" was threatened.
The final version of the Act, through the good offices of Harrison G. Otis, allowed banished aliens to take along their
property.

Likewise, the Sedition Act was defended by Federalists
as a just and reasonable law, more temperate than contemporary English common law practice. In England a citizen charged
with the offense of speaking or printing seditious libel could
not offer evidence of its truth as a defense, nor could he justify
himself with a plea of harmless intent. Some Federalists wanted
identical legislation for the United States, but the Sedition Act
as finally passed contained various safeguards. Anything stated

or published against the national government or any of its officers, which was true, could not be seditious. Even if a statement were false, so the Sedition Act specified, the intent must have been scandalous or malicious to be legally considered a seditious libel. Furthermore, in England the jury could decide only on the facts, that is, only on the question of whether the accused had or had not printed or uttered the statement for which he was charged. The judge had the responsibility of interpreting the law, that is, whether or not the statement was seditious libel. The American Sedition Act allowed the jury to decide on both the fact and the law.

Nevertheless, in operation, these safeguards were of little value. Truth was never used as an effective defense. (In many cases it could not be used for the simple reason that the publications *were* false. But in others the charge involved a spoken or printed opinion that, though perhaps scurrilous, was personal and could not always be supported with documentation.) Lack of malicious intent was also difficult to prove, especially before Federalist judges who assumed base motivations upon the part of all Republicans. On occasion many of these judges freely delivered blazing lectures to the jury, intimidating them into voting for a verdict of guilty. Worst of all was the climate of fear and defiance which the Alien and Sedition Acts aroused. Yet, to the end of their rule many Federalists remained convinced that discontent was caused largely by a want of proper information.

After the Republican victory of 1801, and with the steady growth of democratic thought and practice in the nineteenth century, the Alien and Sedition Acts were thoroughly repudiated. (In fact, the national government did not enact another peace-time sedition statute until 1940.) No lingering Federalist politician publicly raised his voice to defend their wisdom or validity. Quite the contrary, many Federalists—or their biographers—sought to deny or excuse themselves from any personal responsibility for the Alien and Sedition Acts. But historians today agree that virtually all Federalist leaders were culpable. John Adams's public addresses fed the hysteria that swept the country. Only under conditions of fear could the Alien and Sedition Acts have been passed. Hamilton had opposed an early draft of the Sedition law, but then criticized Adams for not enforcing the Act more vigorously. "Are laws of this kind passed merely to excite odium and remain a dead letter?" asked Hamilton. "If the President requires to be stimulated, those who can approach him ought to do it." George Washington endorsed them without qualification. John Marshall stated that had he been in Congress, he would have voted against the Alien and Sedition Acts (for which statement he was roundly condemned by other Federalists). But Marshall redeemed himself in Federalist eyes by providing his party with perhaps the best analysis of the constitutionality of the Acts.

American experience in the mid-twentieth century has changed the opinion of some scholars on the subject of the Alien and Sedition Acts. "Those unhappy measures were neither unconstitutional," writes Page Smith (*John Adams,* 1962), "nor, strictly interpreted, inimical to freedom of the press. They were simply impolitic." England at the same period, and for the same reasons, was the scene of far greater repressions of civil liberties. Scores of historians have written of a reign of terror in America, though of the dozens arrested but fourteen indictments were returned under the Sedition Act. Most were against newspaper printers or publishers, and only ten resulted in conviction. "We can leave the Alien and Sedition Acts to the periodic indignation of righteous historians," says Page Smith, "who will be happy if their own nation and their own times show no grosser offenses against human freedom."

Naturally Republicans were appalled and alarmed at the Alien and Sedition Acts, which they regarded as the most tyrannous of all Federalist measures. Jefferson was no more pleased than Federalists with the scurrilous press. He never regarded, Dumas Malone states (*Jefferson and His Time,* 1948-62), "freedom of political expression as an absolute." But he believed seditious libel prosecutions should be confined to state authority, and should not be used for the purpose of eradicating political opposition. (For a view opposite to that of Dumas Malone, see Leonard Levy, *Jefferson and Civil Liberties: The Darker Side,* 1963). In a sense, Jefferson deemed the Alien and Sedition Acts a crucial test of national character. If the American people were dupes enough to accept this legislation without protest, then there was no hope for democracy. The next step would be an act of Congress proclaiming Adams president for life. The duty of the Republican party, therefore, was to arouse and stimulate the people against these measures. As Republican editors were jailed, more Republican newspapers were started. Hundreds of Republican petitions of protest flooded Congress from towns all over America. Jefferson and Madison, respectively, secretly wrote the famous Kentucky and Virginia resolutions.

The Kentucky resolution was introduced by John Breckenridge and adopted by the state legislature on November 16, 1798. It declared that the Alien and Sedition Acts had violated several parts of the Constitution, particularly the first and fifth amendments. It rang out a challenge "that these and successive acts of the same character, unless arrested on the threshold, may tend to drive these States into revolution and blood, and will furnish new calumnies against Republican governments, and new pretexts for those who wish it to be believed, that man cannot be governed but by a rod of iron." It contained the Jeffersonian theory of strict constitutional construction: that all powers not specifically given to the central government are reserved to the states. For these reasons, the resolution argued, the Alien and Sedition Acts were "unauthoritative, void, and of no force." But the section politicians later quoted so effectively referred to the American government as a compact of the states, and "as in all other cases of compact among parties having no common Judge, *each party has an equal right to judge for itself, as well of infractions as of the mode and measure of redress.*"

The Kentucky resolution in particular (Madison's Virginia resolution, more carefully composed, was less radical) appears to represent a shift in Republican position from a defense of states' rights to the Antifederalist theory of the primacy of state sovereignty. The former accepts the Constitution as a document of and by all the people, creating by its own definition a national government of supreme sovereignty, but clearly and expressly limited to the exercise of particular powers. The latter, called the "compact theory," accepts the Constitution as the work of sovereign states creating a national government which is the agent of and not paramount to the states. Constitutional historians have never agreed on whether the Virginia and Kentucky resolutions should be taken as a statement of basic Republican theory, or whether they should be considered as a political tactic only. Probably, like the colonials of 1763-76, trying to define their position within the British empire, and being driven by parliamentary legislation to ever more radical interpretations, so Jefferson and Madison were attempting to live within the Constitution, but were forced by Federalist authoritarianism to more radical definitions as a measure of self-defense of individual liberties. "It was liberty that Jefferson and Madison were concerned with," historian Henry S. Commager has concluded, "not constitutional doctrine."

If the Sedition Act represents the crest of Federalist extremism, so in the Kentucky resolution Thomas Jefferson "went further in his emphasis on the rights and powers of the states vis-à-vis the general government than he had ever done before," states Dumas Malone, "or was ever to do again." The history of these resolutions, and of supplements passed in 1799 and 1800, as reported by Adrienne Koch and Harry Ammon (in Mrs. Koch's *Jefferson and Madison,* 1950), reveals that Jefferson's more impetuous character was moderated by Madison's tempered reason. Jefferson would have stressed a Republican determination "to sever ourselves from that union we so much value, rather than give up the rights of self government." At Madison's insistence this phrase was withdrawn. Without Madison's calm and judicious advice Jefferson might have raised the doctrines of the Kentucky resolution—that a state legislature could declare an act of Congress null and void—to a binding Republican policy. Jefferson, however, recognized and followed the good sense of Madison's cautious logic.

Jefferson's goal must be understood. His primary desire was not to aggrandize state power, but to protect human liberty. Even Jefferson recognized that Republican strategy had to remain flexible. We should "leave the matter in such a train," Jefferson wrote to Madison, "as that we may not be committed absolutely to push the matter to extremities, and yet may be free to push as far as events will render prudent." But once the ghost of the "compact theory" was raised in the Kentucky and Virginia resolutions, it haunted American history for decades. John C. Calhoun elaborated upon it to provide a permanent defense of Southern slavocracy. The South used it to justify secession in 1861.

It is ironical that Jefferson and Madison should be remembered as founders of a doctrine used by Southern secessionists. They should more justly be recalled as men whose every action in the 1790's was directed to resist such a course, despite repeated insults and injuries to the spirit of republicanism. To these men, Hamilton tried to corrupt that spirit through his economic program; Adams tried to enslave it through the Alien and Sedition Acts. If Federalist measures were left unchallenged, the Constitution would be perverted, and Americans would repeat the European experience of kings, wars, standing armies, an established church, and burdensome taxes. If Federalists were overthrown, the Constitution could then become, as it was originally meant to be, a vehicle to preserve and to strengthen republicanism. The means to do this rested with the people. Jefferson underscored the lesson of Napoleon's *coup d'état* in a letter to his neighbor William Bache: "[Americans] should see in it a necessity to rally firmly and in close bands round their Constitution. Never to suffer an iota of it to be infringed. *To inculcate on minorities the duty of acquiescence in the will of the majority; and on majorities a respect for the rights of the minority.*"

The final irony of the 1790's is that it was Adams, now scorned by Jefferson, who stymied Hamilton's military plans to raise a large army, possibly to be used in a show of strength against Virginia. Historians have never been certain as to Hamilton's intentions. The ostensible reason for the army was as a defense against possible invasion by the French, but the real purpose, wrote Henry Adams, was to employ "such powers in case of domestic difficulties then fully expected to occur." Samuel E. Morison has disagreed with this view: "This indictment, that the regular and provisional armies were designed primarily to suppress democracy, and not to protect the country against France, is not supported by the slightest evidence." Manning Dauer (*The Adams Federalists,* 1953), sides with Henry Adams. He compares Hamilton's desire to use force, and its possible consequences, with Bismarck's policies in Germany after 1862: "Liberalism . . . was defeated, and a military character given to the new state." Stephen Kurtz ("John Adams" in *America's Ten Greatest Presidents,* 1961) feels that Hamilton's "dislike for the Republican party of Jefferson and Madison grew intense, so extreme that he was willing to contemplate military actions against the Southern states. During the winter of 1798-99 the United States passed through a severe constitutional crisis that brought civil war perilously near."

Even if this interpretation is incorrect (John C. Miller, among others, has registered a strong dissent) the fact remains that Adams blocked the military plans of the Hamiltonian clique. Adams was vain, thin-skinned, tactless, dogmatic, and all his life felt unappreciated; but he was also an undesigning and honest man, certain of his views and strong enough to follow them. If he bruised easily, he also displayed a remarkable fortitude. Adams believed that additional army forces were unnecessary and uneconomical. He preferred to augment the navy —and he wished to forestall Hamilton's ambitions. Thus he purposely delayed by neither signing recruitment orders for enlisted men, nor signing commissions for officers. This disagreement between Adams and Hamilton, according to John Quincy Adams, marked the "first decisive symptom" of a schism in the ranks of the Federal party.

Furthermore, it was Adams who thwarted the high Federalists, many of whom wanted a declaration of war after the XYZ Affair, and sent a peace mission to France. It was Adams who defied and stripped Hamilton of the national influence he possessed under Washington. These actions split the Federalist party and contributed to Jefferson's victory in 1801. Adams had courageously placed country before party. "He had performed a pure political act, an act that was sacrificial," states his latest biographer, Page Smith, "an act that Thucydides or Tacitus or Polybius would have applauded." And yet, so bitter were his relations with Jefferson, that Adams left the capital early in the morning of March 4, 1801, to avoid attending the ceremony of Jefferson's inauguration.

There had been many threats of disunion by both parties during the administration of John Adams. But no threat was ever fulfilled. No revolution was announced. No state seceded.

No alien groups were persecuted. No one was shot. No armies marched. Because Adams stood firmly for peace, writes Stephen Kurtz (*The Presidency of John Adams*, 1957), "he put an abrupt end to the plans of the vindictive, militaristic faction that had seized control of the Federalist party." The possible recourse to force to stop political opposition never occurred. Because Jefferson and Madison built the party of opposition as a counter to Federalistic authoritarianism, the nation passed safely through its ordeal of liberty.

Common sense and moderation ultimately prevailed in every case. The apogee of "rightist" extremism was the Alien and Sedition Acts, which most scholars admit were unwise but constitutional. The apogee of "leftist" extremism was the Virginia and Kentucky resolutions which, after all, were expressions of opinion rather than calls to action. As Madison explained in 1800, the Acts were "unaccompanied with any other effect than what they may produce on opinion by exciting reflection." In a sense, both parties had sought out and tested the far boundaries of the Constitution. For the guidance of posterity they had set the liberal and conservative (but hardly the radical) limits of the American political tradition.

THE DEVELOPMENT OF PARTIES

"On the preservation of parties," wrote a Maryland "Farmer" in 1788, "public liberty depends. Whenever men are unanimous on great public questions, whenever there is but one party, freedom ceases and despotism commences." But to most contemporaries the growth of parties was abhorrent. Parties were divisive in effect, and politicians often unscrupulous, corrupt, and self-seeking. The evil seemed to outweigh the good, and party development on a national level, unforeseen by the Founding Fathers, only served to multiply the dangers of this "natural disease of popular governments." Neither Federalist nor Republican seemed to understand that parties, though extraconstitutional, fulfilled an indispensible function in the maintenance of representative government. Jefferson once said: "If I could not go to heaven but with a party, I would not go there at all."

Party organization was in its infancy in the early 1790's, without the disciplined network linking local chapters to a national directorate. All important political spokesmen of the early national period, including the very founders of the Federalist and Republican parties, decried the sad necessity of party action, the ugly results of party spirit. Hamilton insisted that he did not commence political counteractions until he had become "unequivocally convinced of the following truth: that Mr. Madison, co-operating with Mr. Jefferson, is at the head of a faction decidedly hostile to me and my administration." Parties were like wars, evil but sometimes unavoidable, and each side blamed the other for firing the first shot. Like opposing military forces, they were certain of the correctness of their respective positions.

Without a doubt the immediate precursor of and catalyst to party growth was Hamilton's financial program of 1790-91. A sharp and rancorous sectional division in congressional voting occurred on each issue. For example, in the second ballot on assumption, members from the Northern states voted 24 to 9 in approval, while congressmen from the South opposed it 18 to 10. However, four of the latter ten represent changed votes, the result of Jefferson's and Madison's arrangement with Hamilton. The division on excise resulted in a vote of Northern delegations in favor 28 to 6 (four of the latter from Pennsylvania), and Southerners opposed 15 to 7. Finally, on the bill to create a national bank, Northern representatives voted affirmatively 33 to 1, and Southern representatives voted negatively 19 to 6.

It must not be assumed, however, that the two parties

which developed in the next few years were completely sectional. If the Republicans came to count most of their support in the South and West, yet they attempted with marked success to win adherents in the middle-Atlantic and New England states. The Virginia-New York intra-party alliance crystallized in the 1790's, and soon came to dominate Republican inner councils —and much of American politics—for more than a century. Burr's superbly coordinated political machine in New York City, victorious over the Hamiltonians in 1800, provided the foundation for Jefferson's election to the presidency. Even in solidly Federalist areas the steady growth of Republican minorities was impressive. In 1796 Jefferson had little strength in New England. By 1800 Republicans won half of the Massachusetts congressional delegation.

If the Federalists relied mainly on the Northern bloc of states, they were not without champions elsewhere. Two treaties ratified during Washington's second administration helped to gain the support of Westerners. Jay's Treaty, by removing the British from the frontier posts, signified the cessation of Indian raids and the opening of the Northwest to farmer and land speculator. Pinckney's Treaty, by opening navigation of the Mississippi River through Spanish territory, was a vital economic boon to trans-Appalachian frontiersmen. The West remained an unruly region, generally Republican at election time, and with strong separatist tendencies. Nevertheless, the effect of the Jay and Pinckney treaties was to win over a small but steadfast minority of western conservatives to the cause of Federalism. In the South also, Federalism was far from dead, and on occasion displayed vigorous recuperative abilities. Hamilton enjoyed powerful connections with influential South Carolina leaders. Virginia Federalists looked to George Washington and John Marshall, and even Madison's apostasy was later offset by Patrick Henry's conversion to the Federalist cause.

On an economic or class, rather than a geographic, basis,

the same type of rough divisions—with marked exceptions—can be made. For example, it is to some extent true that the commercial classes were generally Federalist, while Republican power was derived mainly from agrarian sections. But to cite one deviation, the port of Wilmington, Delaware, was a Jeffersonian stronghold, while the two southern counties of that state, made up of small-scale, self-sufficient agricultural units, remained solidly Federalist well into the nineteenth century. The sweeping Beardian thesis that Federalists represented the commercial-shipping-financial interests, and Republicans the farmer-planter-slaveholder interests, is of limited validity. Federalist support was much broader than Hamilton's program would indicate. A pro-Beardian scholar, Manning Dauer, has demonstrated that many farmers were more loyal to Adams than to Hamilton and remained Federalist until the imposition of a land tax program in 1798-99, occasioned by the quasi-war with France, drove them into Republican columns. Many urban workers voted Federalist until the highly effective Democratic Societies (organized in 1793, and patterned after the French Jacobin clubs) linked eastern "mechanics" to the cause of Republicanism. One cannot interpret the party split in strictly economic terms. Hamilton's financial program did initiate partisan divisions which took shape in the form of parties. But a host of other equally significant factors influenced American voting behavior.

Some remained Federalist, despite economic considerations, out of loyalty to George Washington. During his second administration Federalists capitalized upon the popular veneration of Washington by labeling Republican criticisms of the President as scandalous and seditious. Some voting patterns were correlated with religious persuasion. Congregationalists, especially in Connecticut, were the most rabid of Federalists; Baptists in Rhode Island were Republican. Older Catholic families in Maryland were Federalist; new Catholic immigrants flocking to urban centers were Republican. Some voted, not on the basis of issues at all, but rather for well-known local figures. The same South Carolina district continued to support Robert Goodloe Harper, although he switched from Republican to staunch Federalist. To some, local problems were of paramount significance. The fact that Federalists insisted on the efficacy of a standing army struck a responsive chord in certain western Carolina and Georgia areas where Indian raids were common. The list of factors to explain voting behavior and party allegiances in the 1790's is complex. The broadest view, that the Hamilton-Jefferson division was mirrored in the nation, that the two parties reflected a geographic and economic split, is correct only within the limitations suggested above.

By far the most important single force in hastening the growth of national parties were American relations with England and France. When news of the French revolution first arrived in 1789, public sentiment was nearly unanimous in its warm endorsement. But as that revolution turned to violence, the conservative sectors of American society became increasingly hostile to its methods and principles. By 1793, when France declared war upon England, it had become an axiom of Federalist belief and a tactic of their politics to condemn both the ideas and the sympathizers of the French government. John Adams once compared the American and French revolutions in one line: "Ours was resistance to innovation; theirs was innovation itself." Neither life nor property were safe in a revolution that, to Federalists, bred not liberty, equality, and fraternity, but atheism, despotism, and imperialism. The virtues of the English system, on the other hand, could be viewed more dispassionately by Federalists who were no longer rebels. The mother country, after all, was the birthplace of Anglo-Saxon laws and institutions—stable, orderly, well-balanced between aristocratic rule and democratic privileges.

Republican convictions were diametrically opposite to the

Federalists. They equated the French with the American revolution, for the purpose of both had been the overthrow of monarchy. The Declaration of Rights, like the Declaration of Independence, meant that the French people were joined with Americans in humanity's march to achieve the inevitable golden age of freedom. Federalists might admire Edmund Burke, but Republicans kept faith with Thomas Paine. England, to them, was the stepmother country, home of the hoary common law and an entrenched upper class. Its high-handed depredations of American commerce were but one irritating manifestation of its conceit.

Soon after the outbreak of the war between England and France, upon the advice of Jefferson, Hamilton, and other cabinet officers, Washington issued a proclamation of neutrality. Such a policy seemed the only logical course (as it does today for many "nonaligned" countries) for a new nation that hoped to preserve its national identity. A legal position of neutrality, however, even for those who subscribed to it, could not erase personal biases. Occasionally Hamilton's pro-British and Jefferson's pro-French sentiments led to respective indiscretions for which both have been condemned by historians. When the French minister, "Citizen" Edmond Genêt, arrived in Philadelphia in 1793 after his triumphant tour from Charleston, Washington had already issued the proclamation. Yet, Jefferson, as Secretary of State, did nothing to stop Genêt's dispatch of secret agents to the American West to organize attacks upon Spanish and British territory. A year later John Jay was sent to London with the difficult task of concluding a treaty with the British. Hamilton, then Secretary of the Treasury, revealed to the English minister the fact that the United States had no intention of joining the anti-British league of armed neutrality.

Neither Jefferson's nor Hamilton's lapses of judgment proved crucial. Genêt soon disgraced himself by antagonizing almost the entire government, including Jefferson. Rather than return to France as a failure, perhaps to be guillotined, Genêt requested and received asylum in the United States. Jay found the British to be more cordial than expected, and concluded a pact which, although unpopular on both sides of the ocean, was ratified with misgivings.

Jay's Treaty has been of particular interest to scholars, aside from its diplomatic significance, because of its obvious effects on domestic politics and the development of parties. Soon after ratification, when the contents of the treaty were broadcast by the Republican editor Benjamin Bache, an uproar ensued. For another two months Washington mulled over the question of relative consequences before he finally signed the Senate's ratification. Thereafter he was subjected to a campaign of vilification in newspapers, pamphlets, and speeches. Hamilton, writing under the pen name "Camillus," defended the treaty, but his retirement from office meant that he could no longer serve as a buffer for political abuse. Dr. Nathaniel Ames wished the President's "hand had been cut off when his glory was at its height, before he blasted all his laurels." These attacks infuriated Washington, convinced him that rampant pro-French factionalism was the prime danger to American unity, and hastened his long-felt desire to return to the quiet of Mount Vernon.

Having lost in the Senate, Republican strategy was to block the appropriations which the House of Representatives had to enact (the amount totalled only $90,000) in order to give effect to Jay's Treaty. Jefferson, titular head of the Republicans ever since his retirement as Secretary of State, was then at Monticello. Madison and his chief lieutenant, William Branch Giles, kept Jefferson fully informed of party tactics and developments. Republicans held a congressional caucus, the first in American history, to decide upon a political rebuttal when Washington refused to abide by a House resolution requesting that he submit the diplomatic papers relating to Jay's Treaty.

Hamilton was also busy. He marshalled the support of Northern businessmen in defense of Washington and the treaty. Soon a flood of Federalist-inspired petitions and memorials inundated Congress. Public opinion, which had been predominantly antipathetic to the treaty, now seemed to oscillate as many people had second thoughts. The Republican advantage was canceled. On May 1, 1796, Congress, again by a sectional vote, passed the appropriation bill 51 to 48.

It is difficult to say precisely why the Republicans were defeated in this vote. The change in public opinion probably had some effect, as did the dramatic speech of Fisher Ames delivered shortly before the final vote. (See Winfred Bernhard, *Fisher Ames*, 1965.) There were also Federalist threats to reject ratification of Pinckney's Treaty, and even to destroy the union, unless the lower House voted for the appropriation. Under these pressures Madison could not keep some Republicans from abandoning the party position. "For the moment at least," a disappointed Madison wrote to James Monroe of the result, "it presses hard on the republican interest."

In the long run, though Madison could not foresee it, Jay's Treaty benefited the Republicans. Party ranks shifted as various conservatives, particularly in the South, abandoned the Federalists and took up the Republican cause. Party ranks tightened as the "British treaty" became an issue in the election of 1796. Party spirits heightened, for with Washington's retirement the voter was given a clear choice between Jefferson and Adams. Party machinery continued its course of development from congressional origins to national forms. To be sure, the existence of parties was still largely deplored, but the criticisms now seemed to come more often from Federalist than from Republican sources. A large part of Washington's Farewell Address in 1796, which warned against the "baneful effects" of parties, was really directed against Republicans only. A few years earlier, Jefferson would have agreed with the philosophy of Washington's message, but no longer. He now defended the necessity of vigorous party action, at least in the United States. On the last day of December, 1795, he wrote to William Branch Giles: "Were parties here divided merely by a greediness for office, as in England, to take part with either would be unworthy of a reasonable or moral man, but where the principle of difference is as substantial and as strongly pronounced as between the republicans and the Monocrats of our country, I hold it as immoral to pursue a middle line, as between parties of Honest men and Rogues, into which every country is divided."

Jefferson had no desire to be president in 1797. His nomination was unsought, the work of Republican leaders in Congress who did not even consult him. "There is nothing I so anxiously hope," he hold Madison, "as that my name may come out either second or third." To Edward Rutledge he repeated: "I protest before my god, that I shall, from the bottom of my heart, rejoice at escaping." Part of this reluctance is explained by Jefferson's delight in the private role of gentleman farmer; but part also, in his shrewd and accurate guess that the following four years would be perilous with unresolved questions. Jay's Treaty would not keep the British from illegal search and seizures of American ships, or from impressment of American sailors. Moreover, the treaty convinced the French that the United States was now allied to Britain. France was bound to show her displeasure. The next president would inherit these problems from the Washington administration. "This is certainly not a moment to covet the helm," said Jefferson.

Without Washington's prestige, without a first-rate cabinet, and with a victory margin of only three electoral votes, John Adams faced the problem of steadily deteriorating Franco-American relations from the moment of his inauguration. In the West Indies, American ships were seized by the French and their cargoes confiscated. The government of France decreed that American citizens found serving on British vessels (whether they were impressed or not seemed immaterial) would be hung if captured. Charles C. Pinckney, the minister to France sent to replace James Monroe, was not received. In fact, he was insulted by the French and commanded to leave their country. Confronted with such bellicose measures, Adams adopted a policy of continued negotiations for a peaceful arrangement with the French, but lest diplomacy fail, he also recommended preparations for war.

A special mission of three men, Pinckney of South Carolina, Elbridge Gerry of Massachusetts, and John Marshall of Virginia, was appointed to treat with France. As everyone realized, upon the outcome of the mission there undoubtedly depended the question of peace or war with France, our future relations with England, and public support in the next elections for either the Federalist or the Republican party. Mail from Europe was anxiously awaited for some news of the negotiations. Dark hints and ugly rumors multiplied, many to the effect that the American ministers had been humiliated. At this time a Federalist in Congress spoke of the Republicans as "a well organized and disciplined Corps, never going astray, or doing right even by mistake."

But the Republicans did make a mistake. They insisted upon seeing the diplomatic dispatches, and even the astute Albert Gallatin and the wily William Branch Giles could not dissuade their fellow partisans from voting for a House resolution requesting the papers. Adams was only too happy to oblige, for here was "proof as strong as Holy Writ" of French insult and corruption such as to arouse the indignation of every loyal American citizen. Marshall, Pinckney, and Gerry were never officially received by the French foreign minister, Talleyrand. Instead, they were contacted by his agents who demanded a large personal bribe, a substantial monetary "loan" for the French government, and a public apology for the anti-French remarks of President Adams. When Adams read the report he thought of war. The Federalists were rejuvenated. The Republicans, reported Fisher Ames, "were confounded, and the trimmers dropt off from the party like windfalls from an apple tree in September."

Many Republican congressmen simply packed up and went home. A wave of patriotic fervor, of pent-up nationalism, of anti-Gallic sentiment, swept the nation. Addresses of support flooded in on Adams from literally hundreds of towns and cities and from all classes of society. Joseph Hopkinson wrote the words for the occasion, and overnight "Hail Columbia" replaced "Ça ira." The French tricolored cockade did not disappear entirely, but more black ones indicating support of the government were in evidence. Adams, busy enough answering the testimonials, took time to proclaim a day of "Public Humiliation, Fasting and Prayer Throughout the United States." Subscriptions to Republican newspapers fell off disastrously. "If these papers fall," Jefferson told Madison, "republicanism will be entirely browbeaten." Worst of all were the results of the 1798-99 elections. The Federalist majority in the lower House rose to an estimated twenty, and this gain came largely from the South.

If Jefferson was dismayed, still the Republican cause was far from hopeless. The season had come, he said early in 1799, "for systematic energies and sacrifices." In the next few years Jefferson provided his party with both strategy and platform: the Alien and Sedition Acts must be repealed, and freedom of the press restored; the military must be disbanded and reliance for internal defense placed squarely and solely upon the militia; the navy was too expensive and must be reduced to a size sufficient only to guard our coasts from invasion; the engrossment of power by the national government must cease, and a true federal balance be restored; no preference for any foreign nation must be shown, and peace must be maintained with all; commerce must be open with all countries, but political alliances with none; the public debt must be retired; and government must be frugal. "These . . . are my principles," said Jefferson, "[and] they are unquestionably the principles of the great body of our fellow citizens." To accomplish these goals the Republican party had to exert itself to win the election of 1800. To stop Jefferson's election became the aim of all Federalists.

Everywhere, though in varying degrees, party machinery was organized more efficiently. Caucuses were held, corresponding committees appointed, newspapers subsidized to support either Federalists or Republicans. Rather remarkable transformations had taken place in political attitudes and practices since the inception of the Constitution a decade before. "Far reaching changes," writes Noble E. Cunningham, who has spelled them out, "had been ushered into the political life of the United States." Campaigning, which once had been denounced as improper, increased to such an extent that it became socially acceptable in most regions. Similarly, many candidates who once had boasted of their independent judgment, now found it an asset to speak of their firm and steady allegiance to party. Tickets became common and voters were advised to consider the good of the party as superior to the personal characteristics of a candidate. More people actively participated in politics than ever before and were urged to do so by local leaders. If, as Carl R. Fish once noted, politics became the passion of the nineteenth century American, the great awakening started in the 1790's.

These changes in practice and organization presaged a new appreciation of political parties. "In every free and deliberating society," Jefferson wrote to John Taylor in 1798, "there must, from the nature of man, be opposite parties and violent dissensions and discords, and one of these, for the most part must prevail over the other for a longer or shorter time. Perhaps this party division is necessary to induce each to watch and relate to the people the proceedings of the other."

From statements such as this Saul K. Padover (*Jefferson,* 1942) has concluded that Jefferson "was one of the first great modern leaders to realize that political parties were essential to self-government." Yet, the old distrust never quite died. In fact, it is still very much a part of the American character to view politics and politicians with some distaste. Even Jefferson's acknowledgment of the indispensable role of political parties to democracy was temporary. Shortly after he became president, Jefferson expressed the hope that parties, having served their purpose, would wither away.

In the balance, Federalist mistakes were as significant as Republican efforts for the final outcome of the election of 1800. The Alien and Sedition Acts were unpopular, an easy target for Republican orators. The Federalist tax program surely did not win friends. But more important than any other single reason for the Republican victory was the split that developed within the Federalist party. When Adams's earlier belligerency changed, and he chose to send a new peace mission to France in 1799, the ark of Federalism cracked. Then, when in May, 1800, he dismissed the Hamiltonians in his cabinet, the breach became irreparable. Hamilton campaigned openly for Pinckney, and wrote a widely distributed pamphlet attacking Adams. Republicans rejoiced, nodded knowingly, and quoted the maxim: "When thieves fall out, honest men come by their own."

Adams was narrowly defeated, but the results were complicated by a tied electoral vote between the Republican candidates, Jefferson and Aaron Burr. A choice between the two fell, by constitutional provision, upon the House of Representatives. And there—despite Hamilton's impassioned and desperate advice to his political comrades that they support Jefferson as the lesser evil—Federalists voted unanimously for Burr. The Republicans just as adamantly remained loyal to Jefferson. Thirty-five times a vote was taken and neither party could obtain the necessary plurality. Political passions soared during this stalemate, for without a constitutionally elected president by inauguration date, the Constitution must perish. Hamilton was powerless. The Federalist members of Congress, acting in a phalanx, were positive that Jefferson would destroy the national government anyway. Why not resist this eventuality by supporting Burr, and hope the Republican forces would crack under pressure? But Republicans remained firm, their resolve steeled by the Federalists' obvious thwarting of the majority will. Finally a few Federalists, led by James A. Bayard of Delaware, could no longer follow the logic of their party. They cast blank ballots, thereby giving the election to Jefferson. The significance of those blank ballots looms large in American history. "For a season it seemed as though the Republican party was to be denied the right to exist as a legal opposition, entitled to obtain power by persuasion," Allen Johnson has stated. "They won, therefore, for all time, that recognition of the right of legal opposition which is the primary condition of successful popular government."

TWO

Republican Domination, 1801-1815

JEFFERSON IN POWER

To Federalist leaders Thomas Jefferson was the political devil incarnate, sworn to dismantle the governmental handiwork so carefully constructed in the past decade. Slowly but surely, they predicted, the proud Virginian would restore power to the states at the expense of the central authority. He would ally the United States to France, and America would experience its own reign of terror. He would undermine the Federalist bases of prosperity, and property values would tumble. What would be left of the republic when Jefferson finished his diabolical schemes? The army and navy would be reduced to impotence. Under the guise of economy even the United States Mint would be eliminated. Commerce would suffer. Judicial independence would be prostrated. Organized religion would be assaulted. To complete the work Jefferson would probably involve the United States in a war with Great Britain. The Constitution could not withstand this attack and remain an effective document. But most galling, at least to Northern Federalists, was Jefferson's hypocrisy. He was a slave-owning plantation aristocrat posing as a democratic friend of the masses. He was a demagogue whose aim was personal power, and he obtained votes by preaching ideas to the electorate that he did not personally practice. At least, said the Federalists, they had never stooped to these methods. They had never appealed to the baser instincts of human beings in order to win office.

Many Republicans also regarded the electoral triumph of 1801 as a revolution, but in the technical rather than the common meaning of that term: as a complete circling back to original practices. Certainly Jefferson did not interpret his victory as a mandate for radical innovations in government. Quite the contrary, it was his firm belief that the Federalists had misused the Constitution to create a "monocratic" system (he invented the word) inimical to democracy. They, not the Republicans, were the innovators. Jefferson admitted that some Federalist legacies could not easily be uprooted, after a ten-year growth, without some danger to the economic structure of the country. Nor did he have a positive program of legislation ready to substitute for the Federalist one. In general, he thought that human freedom and national welfare would be served by simply removing a number of Federalist laws and practices. The effect of this might be regarded as "revolutionary." But actually, progress would be achieved—to paraphrase Jefferson, who preferred nautical metaphors—by steering the ship of state back to a straightforward Republican path.

Above all the nation needed some respite from the partisanship which had divided Americans ever since the beginning of the Hamiltonian program. Bitterness and emotional wrangling had replaced understanding and calm discussion. Friendships of long standing had broken under the strain. Politicians distrusted and had often insulted one another. The party press had reached extremes of licentiousness. Jefferson's inaugural speech, therefore, was a peace offering. "We have called by different names brethren of the same principle," he stated. "We are all republicans—we are all federalists."

At first Jefferson anticipated the end of political parties, but soon realized that such an expectation was illusory. He found that he could not gain the trust of Federalist leaders. Their enmity seemed intransigent, as immutable as a law of nature. But he hoped the bulk of their followers might unite with Republicans on the basis of common American principles.

Unlike his predecessors Jefferson consciously wore the two faces of his office: president of the United States and recognized leader of his party. He tried to remain faithful and to advance the cause of both, for which he was roundly condemned. Despite the buffeting, and despite some troubling exceptions to the contrary, Jefferson was not generally aware of any particular dichotomy between his dual roles. He equated the aims of the Republican party with the good of the majority of the American people, and he fulfilled both roles expeditiously and diplomatically. Few of the presidents who came after Jefferson, in the judgment of William N. Chambers (*Political Parties in a New Nation: The American Experience,* 1963), "were to prove as apt and determined as he did in party leadership and legislative influence, [or] as successful in party government."

He was, in short, a superb politician. For example, he knew

that the Republican party was not strong enough in the North. Especially in New England it was distrusted as a tool of Southerners. For ten years Federalist pamphleteers and ministers, who freely mixed their religion with politics, penned essays on the economic and moral superiority of the North contrasted to Southern decadence. Even more significant than the issue of morality was the constitutional compromise whereby three-fifths of the slaves were counted for purposes of representation. A moderate, normally level-headed individual like John Quincy Adams complained that "Every planter south of the Potomac has three votes in effect for every five slaves he keeps in bondage, while a New England farmer, who contributes tenfold as much to the support of the Government, has only a single vote." Jefferson had to overcome this bias to wean Northern voters away from their traditional allegiance to Federalism. One of his initial moves in selecting a cabinet was to include two New Englanders, Levi Lincoln and Henry Dearborn of Massachusetts, for the respective posts of Attorney General and Secretary of War. The position of Postmaster General, not then considered of cabinet rank, was awarded to Gideon Granger of Connecticut.

Granger often reported to Jefferson on party developments in New England. The work was hard, especially in Connecticut, where one Republican organizer complained that "The priesthood are armed against us with all the powers of their order." Despite these difficulties, according to Noble Cunningham (*The Jeffersonian Republicans in Power: Party Operations,* 1963), "there was more extensive development of Republican party machinery in New England than in any other part of the country." Jefferson's patronage policies in Massachusetts helped the Republican organization overcome entrenched Federalist interests. By 1804, as a result of such careful cultivation, Jefferson attracted a majority of Northern voters to the cause of Republicanism. In fact, in the presidential election of that year Jefferson was victorious over his Federalist opponent, Charles C. Pinckney, in every state except Connecticut and Delaware.

Jefferson's skill as a politician is further revealed in his relations with Congress. Republicans commanded a clear majority in both houses, but Jefferson wanted strong administrative spokesmen to enforce party discipline and direct party strategy. James Madison had acted this role in the earliest years of Republican formation and Albert Gallatin had succeeded to the post of minority leader during the presidency of John Adams. Now, with Madison and Gallatin in the cabinet, Jefferson searched for adequate replacements. Talent was not the basic problem, though Jefferson probably wished it were better distributed geographically. Most of the Republican legislators from New England were capable but inexperienced, so that leadership devolved naturally upon the Southern members of the party. Personal discord marred the relations of these Southerners. An early rivalry developed between Nathaniel Macon (Speaker of the House) and William Branch Giles. Later John Randolph, Jr., replaced Giles and despite the best efforts of Jefferson to cooperate with Randolph, by 1806 the latter formed the nucleus of a small anti-administration group in Congress which would not be appeased. Each Republican quarrel was seized upon by Federalist partisans with delight, for they were eager to capitalize upon such divisions.

But they were disappointed. Jefferson never did discover any single brilliant and towering figure who could neutralize Randolph, outwit the Federalists, and unite all loyal Republican legislators. As a matter of fact the Republican majority was generally too large to act as a single, disciplined unit. Some defections were inevitable. Nevertheless, Jefferson did effect a surprising degree of presidential leadership over Congress and, under the circumstances, an extraordinary amount of party cohesion. Sometimes directly, more often through Secretary of the Treasury Albert Gallatin or other cabinet members, ideas for legislation were forwarded to Congress. On occasion Jefferson even sent the draft of a bill, but with a request for secrecy "as he is very unwilling to meddle personally with the details of the proceeding of the legislature." Personal contact was deemed important and Jefferson frequently invited groups of Republican and Federalist congressmen (separately, to be sure) to dine at the executive mansion. Jefferson's "whole system of administration," John Quincy Adams recorded, "seems founded upon this principle of carrying through the legislature measures by his personal or official influence."

From the very beginning of Jefferson's term of office Federalists marshalled their best arguments and finest orators against Republican legislation. They lamented, cajoled, threatened, raved, and broadcast each successive example of Republican perfidy—all to no avail. The Republicans had the votes, and because of Jefferson's political acumen they cooperated in a rare display of party solidarity.

Many laws and customs originated by the Federalists under Washington and Adams were abandoned or transformed according to the Republican tenets of personal liberty, governmental economy, and social simplicity. These were the distinguishing hallmarks of Jeffersonian Republicanism. Internal taxes were either reduced or abolished. The military budget was drastically cut. The Alien and Sedition Acts were permitted to lapse. The maintenance of ministers to Holland, Portugal, and Prussia, deemed unnecessary and too expensive, were withdrawn. Gallatin was instructed to devise a plan to reduce and eventually to extinguish the public debt. He was cautioned by the President to keep "the finances of the Union as clear and intelligible as a merchant's books, so that every member of Congress, and every man of any mind in the Union, should be able to comprehend them. . . ." The elegant levees of previous administrations smacked of European aristocratic practices and were, besides, too costly. The frugal Mr. Jefferson replaced them with comparatively simple receptions.

The Judiciary Act of 1801, passed by the Federalists shortly before they left office, was repealed after a major debate between the two parties. Federalists argued that the law could not be repealed without violating the clear mandate of the Constitution. The basic law of the land guaranteed the tenure of federal judges. So long as they exercised "good Behavior" their salaries could not be diminished nor could they be removed except by the process of impeachment. Republicans responded that Congress had authority, by constitutional provision, over all inferior federal courts. They were the creations of Congress and by logic they could be abolished by Congress. To reason any other way would permit each successive Congress to do exactly what the Federalists had done in 1801: a defeated party could quietly create new judicial posts, sinecures to be filled with their defeated or deserving members. Despite the anguished pleas of Federalists that the federal balance would be destroyed, judicial independence ruined, and the Constitution mortally wounded, the repealing act did no more than effect a return to earlier legislation which had established the federal court system in 1789. The Republican assault on the Federalist judicial fortress was quite conservative. It overthrew, wrote Henry Adams, "a mere outer line of defense."

To Henry Adams, whose nine-volume *History of the United States During the Administrations of Jefferson and Madison* has influenced the views of scholars since it first appeared some seventy-five years ago, the repeal of the judiciary act typified Jefferson's chameleon-like character. For almost a decade Jefferson had railed against the centralization of national power, broad construction, and unrestrained judicial authority. He had long espoused the principles of states' rights and limited government. "The essence of Virginia Republicanism lay in a single maxim," Adams stated: "THE GOVERNMENT SHALL NOT BE THE FINAL JUDGE OF ITS OWN POWERS." One might have expected Jefferson to propose some changes, perhaps in the form of a constitutional amendment defining the "necessary and proper" clause, or making judges removable by the executive on address by the legislature, or checking judicial review by some type of popular referendum. Above all else, wrote Adams: "If the revolution of 1800 was to endure, it must control the Supreme Court." A simple law enlarging the number of justices would have accomplished this purpose. For, unless some such changes were made, then the principles championed by the Republicans were no better than campaign jargon, catchwords to gain power and then be forgotten. "No party could claim the right to ignore its principles at will," according to Adams, "or imagine that theories once dropped could be resumed with equal chance of success." Adams dismissed Jefferson's statesmanship with one line: "Serious statesmen could hardly expect to make a revolution that should not be revolutionary."

Brilliantly, but malevolently, Henry Adams attempted to analyze the reasons for Jefferson's intentional "inaction." Broadly speaking, he offered two confusing, if not contradictory, explanations. First, Adams agreed with Hamilton's characterization of Jefferson as being "likely as any man I know to temporize, to calculate what will be likely to promote his own reputation and advantage; and the probable result of such a temper is the preservation of systems, though originally opposed, which, being once established, could not be overturned without danger to the person who did it." That is to say, Adams saw Jefferson as an essentially conservative individual; yet he ascribed this conservatism, not to convictions courageously maintained, but to Jefferson's assiduous courting of popularity and his refusal to implement any changes that might threaten his position. He viewed Jefferson as a man of expediency, as an egotist whose knowledge was versatile but superficial, as a "martyr to the disease of omniscience." Above all, Jefferson could not resist the temptations of power. Presidential "inaction" was to be explained, fundamentally, by the fact that if Jefferson attempted to apply his principles of the 1790's, he would have divested both himself and the Republican party of the authority they now possessed. Rather than do this, said Adams, Jefferson cynically "stretched out his hand to seize the powers he had [once] denounced."

On the other hand, Adams did allow that perhaps Jefferson's plan to avoid immediate theoretical confrontations with the Federalists was based on his hope of diminishing executive authority and overweening national power by the means of slow and cautious example. His presidential "inaction" would gradually restore a proper federal balance according to true Republican principles. Still, to Adams, the motive could only have been that of a self-seeking politician. He quoted with approval John Marshall's summary opinion of Jefferson: "By weakening the office of President, he will increase his personal power." Besides, Adams reasoned, Jefferson's "inaction" was "certainly intentional." Jefferson cunningly planned to "annihilate the last opposition before attempting radical reforms." This strategy, however, did not work. The task was simply beyond Jefferson's abilities. The exigencies of office, if not his personal inclinations, forced Jefferson to augment rather than to reduce executive authority. The period of initial "inaction" was followed by Jefferson's frank utilization of Federalist practices. In fact, said Adams, "it was hard to see how any President could be more Federalist than Jefferson himself."

For example, Jefferson sent a naval squadron to the Mediterranean on a warlike mission against the Barbary pirates without first requesting the permission of Congress, despite the fact that two of his cabinet officers insisted that such an action was unconstitutional. He supported Gallatin's plan to use federal funds for a vast scheme of internal improvements, a project smacking of Hamiltonianism. He continued his animosity toward the Bank of the United States, yet acquiesced when Gallatin enlarged its influence and utilized its resources. Whatever vigor the Jeffersonian administration possessed, whatever good it accomplished, was achieved by a combination of dexterity and duplicity that employed sound Federalist tactics under a façade of clever Republican rhetoric.

Other scholars have dissented from Adams's biased assessment on the following grounds:

1. It is predicated on viewing Jefferson as an ultra-radical Republican theoretician of the 1790's. William N. Chambers believes it "an overdramatization to characterize them [Republicans] in their years of opposition as though they were virtually an American branch of world-revolutionary Jacobinism, committed to basic social reconstruction." Quite the contrary, Republican leaders in opposition were liberal rather than radical in their determination to preserve republican government; moderate rather than extremist in their means; democratic rather than demagogic in their insistence upon majority rule; and guided usually by common sense more than theoretical considerations in their policy.

2. Jefferson avoided unnecessary ideological conflicts not because he was cowardly, or insincere, or grasping, but because he was a political realist who wished to ease the strains of faction and restore the "fabric of consensus." Thus, though Jefferson disapproved of judicial review, regarding it as undemocratic as well as unconstitutional, his attack on the judiciary was based on political rather than theoretical grounds. The federal courts had become a fortress of the Federalists, their final bastion, and Jefferson quite naturally wanted to flush them out. Albert Beveridge has called this Jeffersonian assault on the courts "one of the really great crises in American history." So it seemed at the time, but actually the courts emerged from their ordeal unscathed and with their influence enhanced.

3. No one can deny that the Republicans in power on occasion amended, compromised, or modified previous views. But this was largely the result of either new circumstances or changed conditions to which every party must adapt, particularly when it assumes office for the first time. To conclude that the Republicans abandoned their tenets, and that they later outfederalized the Federalists, is to miss the enormous consistency between their promises and the fulfillment of those promises. Republican legislation after 1801, William Chambers believes, was a prime example of fidelity to "the tacit or explicit commitments of ideology and policy they had made." No sweeping program of positive social or economic reforms was enacted; but then, none had been proposed. The Republicans were not supposed to innovate, but to undo Federalist innovations. This was the meaning of the "Revolution of 1800." More was not expected.

Yet, the Louisiana Purchase looms as possibly the most important exception to such a thesis, a glaring example of Jefferson and his party assuming a course which clearly violated Republican constitutional scruples. At least so it has been often cited by American historians. The territory had been owned by France until 1763 when it was ceded to Spain, and then retroceded by the secret Treaty of San Ildefonso signed on October 1, 1800. News that France had acquired Louisiana—at first inconclusive, but then undeniable—touched off a series of speculative and nervous reactions in America. The Federalists hoped to capitalize on what they regarded as an insoluble dilemma for the Republican administration. Either Jefferson must declare war against France in order to satisfy the mounting martial fever of the West, or by pursuing a pacific policy, risk unpopularity and a consequent Federalist renaissance. In any case, Federalists believed, Jefferson was caught between two evils.

They introduced a flock of resolutions designed to force his hand. Roger Griswold of Connecticut requested information from the President on the exact nature of the transfer of Louisiana to France. Later, James Ross of Pennsylvania called for the immediate occupation of New Orleans. The Federalists did not really want New Orleans and they were, as a group, opposed to Western interests. But they swallowed their distaste and fixed on a policy to stir up the West and use Louisiana as an effective issue in the elections of 1804.

Jefferson was gravely concerned. Imperialistic France in possession of Louisiana was a different matter than feeble Spain. "The day that France takes possession of N. Orleans . . . ," Jefferson had predicted in 1802, "we must marry ourselves to the British fleet and nation." But there was some chance, Pierre duPont suggested, that France might be persuaded to sell New Orleans. Congress authorized an appropriation of two million dollars for this purpose, and James Monroe was dispatched as minister extraordinary to join Robert R. Livingston in Paris for the negotiations. If these failed, the American diplomats were instructed to proceed across the channel and sign a treaty of alliance with Great Britain.

Shortly before Monroe arrived in Paris, Napoleon had decided to rid himself of the entire Louisiana Territory. His losses in Santo Domingo, trying to subdue the Negro revolutionaries, were catastrophic. In 1802 alone, approximately fifty thousand French soldiers died in battle or from yellow fever. Without Santo Domingo pacified, and thus productive, Louisiana had little value to the French dictator. Besides, war between England and France was imminent. Napoleon could not waste more troops in Santo Domingo, nor send any to occupy and defend Louisiana. He needed money. He realized Louisiana would be vulnerable to British or American seizure the moment war was declared. And he wished to halt and even reverse the growing rapprochement between England and the United States which French possession of Louisiana seemed to foster. "I renounce Louisiana," Napoleon told his ministers. "It is not only

New Orleans that I mean to cede; it is the whole colony, reserving none of it."

Though the American ministers had been provided with a number of alternate possibilities, none covered the purchase of the whole colony. They were unprepared and even mystified by Napoleon's sudden offer. Nevertheless, they recognized the immense value of Louisiana immediately, did not quibble at violating some of Secretary of State James Madison's instructions, and signed the *projet* by which the United States agreed to pay some fifteen million dollars for the territory. Formal ratification had to be accomplished by October 30, 1803. "We have lived long," Robert R. Livingston said to his fellow diplomat Monroe, "but this is the noblest work of our lives."

Contemporary opinion in the United States was equally enthusiastic. Madison was jubilant, calling the purchase "a truly noble acquisition." Jefferson agreed, but his high spirits were tempered by doubts concerning the constitutionality of the treaty. For the Constitution was mute on the question of the United States acquiring territory. Moreover, specific parts of the treaty—for example, the provision that this area would eventually be formed into states, full partners in the federal union—also ran counter to Republican constitutional interpretation. Approval of the treaty would alter, if not destroy, the Republican tenets of limited government and strict construction. It would, in effect, endorse the Hamiltonian concept of implied powers. But approval of the treaty would also eradicate the perennial worry of free navigation of the Mississippi and the right of deposit at New Orleans. It would allay Western discontents, ruin Federalist hopes of regaining office, quiet Indian raids instigated by foreign powers, and free the United States from the necessity of an alliance with England. More significant, the purchase of Louisiana would double the size of the country and open a boundless land to settlement.

In early September, 1803, Jefferson advised Republican leaders to ratify the treaty. He realized, rather remorsefully, that this action would be construed as a precedent for a broad interpretation of the Constitution. "I had rather ask an enlargement of power from the nation, where it is found necessary," he reminded Senator Wilson C. Nicholas of Virginia, "than to assume it by a construction which would make our powers boundless. Our peculiar security is in the possession of a written Constitution. Let us not make it a blank paper by construction." But no time remained for a constitutional amendment permitting the purchase. The treaty had to be approved immediately, wrote Jefferson, "with as little debate as possible, particularly so far as respects the constitutional difficulty." The positive benefits of the Louisiana acquisition justified the means. Besides, Jefferson found some consolation in reflecting that "the good sense of our country will correct the evil of construction when it shall produce ill effects."

If, in the judgment of posterity, Jefferson was right in approving the treaty for the purchase of Louisiana, it does not necessarily invalidate the arguments of the Federalists. As a group they were embittered men who sought mainly to demean the administration, and dreamed only of regaining the powers they possessed before 1801. Federalist motivations in most instances were personal and sectional. Their extremist proposals crossed the limits of the American political tradition. Nevertheless, whatever the fundamental reasons for their opposition to Louisiana, their position was legally and logically sound. "It seems impossible to modern Americans, fully cognizant of what the trans-Mississippi area has contributed to the nation," Lynn Turner has recently commented (*William Plumer of New Hampshire,* 1962), "that men who opposed the annexation of this territory could have been either honest or patriotic. The Federalists were both, even though they may have been mistaken."

To be sure, the Federalists were alarmed at the cost of

Louisiana, which would increase the national debt some fifty per cent. They felt the sudden addition to the union of this vast Western world would surely lessen the political significance of the Northeast. They resurrected the old Antifederalist theme that a republican form of government could not exist over an enormous area. Like Jefferson, but publicly, they questioned whether the treaty power could be stretched to transcend the Constitution itself. But their most telling point involved the validity of the title to Louisiana. For, if by the Treaty of San Ildefonso the land could not be sold or given or transferred to a third party unless certain stipulations were fulfilled, then its sale by France could be regarded as void. The conveyed title would be faulty.

Such, in fact, was the case. The Spanish minister to the United States, the Marquis d'Yrujo, warned "that this [Louisiana] treaty is founded in the breach of faith on the part of that nation [France]." Thus, Federalists in Congress demanded proof that the United States had purchased a clear title and not "a mere quit-claim." Republicans, in rebuttal, could only cite an order of the King of Spain announcing the cession of Louisiana to France. The question was moot and of course perfectly suited to the legal talents of both Federalist and Republican congressmen. Beyond debate, however, was the fact of the continued Spanish possession of Louisiana. What if the Spaniards refused to recognize the Louisiana treaty? Jefferson would then have been in an embarrassing position. Having endorsed the expenditure of fifteen million dollars on a purchase of dubious validity, his sole alternative would have been to invade and fight the Spaniards for possession. Albert Gallatin in fact had suggested military preparations to capture New Orleans in the event that Spain refused to surrender the territory. Jefferson responded by ordering a concentration of troops in the lower Mississippi region. For a moment war seemed to be imminent. "The arrival of the news from Washington," wrote Henry Clay, then practicing law in Kentucky, "relative to the expedition to New Orleans, has called the public attention from every other object. . . . Armies, sieges, and storms completely engross the public mind, and the first interrogatory put on every occasion is: Do you go to New Orleans?"

Jefferson's brinkmanship was successful. On November 30, 1803, in a public ceremony, the Spanish governor turned over control of Louisiana to a French representative who, after holding it for twenty days, transferred it to American hands. In sum, the purchase of Louisiana was an act of calculated boldness. It was a gamble but, given Spain's weakness, neither desperate nor reckless. The achievement crowned Jefferson's first administration. "Without the guilt or calamities of conquest," recorded his eulogist William Wirt, "a vast and fertile region added to our country, far more extensive than her original possessions, bringing along with it the Mississippi and the port of Orleans, the trade of the West to the Pacific Ocean, and in the intrinsic value of the land itself, a source of permanent and almost inexhaustible income."

Some authors have seemed to delight in recording Jefferson's mental anguish when confronted with the Louisiana treaty. They have excoriated Jefferson for inconsistency and present the acquisition as a vindication of Federalist principles. "Jefferson's silence," wrote Richard Hildreth in 1851, "must be considered as amounting to a recantation of the doctrine he had so zealously maintained against Hamilton—a recantation which the whole Republican party joined." Henry Adams stated that the political consequences of the Louisiana treaty were final; nor could Jefferson, in later years, reverse the "fatal error his friends had forced him to commit and which he could neither repudiate nor defend." The writings of Albert Beveridge, biographer of John Marshall, typify the Federalist-oriented genre. Jefferson did not want Louisiana, did not know what to do with it, and was not concerned with the "immorality" of the purchase but merely with the "inconvenience." So, to his infinite dismay, wrote Beveridge, "Jefferson was forced to deal with the Louisiana Purchase by methods as vigorous as any ever advocated by the abhorred Hamilton—methods more autocratic than those which, when done by others, he had savagely denounced as unconstitutional and destructive of liberty."

Other scholars have attempted to redress the imbalances of this anti-Jeffersonian interpretation. To be sure, writes William N. Chambers, the Louisiana windfall did strain Republican principles. But it was fully consistent "with the most basic of the Jeffersonian commitments: their popular-agrarian perspective and its national fulfillment." It should not be forgotten, as historian Henry S. Commager has noted, that Jefferson was the most western-minded of early American statesmen. He envisioned an American empire covering "the whole northern, if not the southern continent, with a people speaking the same language, governed in similar forms, and by similar laws." To gain an empire Jefferson consciously, but he hoped temporarily, abandoned Republican doctrines of strict construction. By so doing he proved to the American people, according to his partisan biographer Henry S. Randall, "that [he was] a great and vigorous statesman guid[ing] the helm of public affairs, instead of the philosophical and visionary theorist who had been described to them." Finally, Jefferson possessed a profound sense of national consciousness. The thread which tied together all of Jefferson's actions was his belief that America was unique in the world and its future must be kept distinct from that of Europe. Thus Jefferson once advised our youth to receive their education at home rather than in European schools, lest they absorb ideas and traits he considered "alarming to me as an American." From *Notes on Virginia* written in 1781 to his advice at the time of Monroe's doctrine in 1822-23, Jefferson thought of America first. The United States was destined for greatness so long as a sharp line isolated her from European infection. That destiny lay through Louisiana to the West. The ultimate meaning of the Jeffersonian administration depends not so much on its constitutional rationalizations as on its manner and spirit and purpose.

FEDERALIST EXTREMISM AND REPUBLICAN SCHISM

The death of the Federalist party was not sudden or dramatic, but slow and painful. A disease of inertia sapped its spirit and vitality. No leader appeared to resist the course. "I will fatten my pigs and prune my trees," declared Fisher Ames, "nor will I any longer . . . trouble to govern this country." Ames had no doubt that the Republican Party would ruin the country, and he took some satisfaction in contemplating and chronicling every sign of catastrophe. Ames typified "the common tendency of Federalist leaders, in consonance with their aristocratic aloofness and dislike of democracy," writes Lynn Turner, ". . . to retire from the field of combat and sulk in their tents when the struggle became too severe." John Adams, also in retirement, felt the same way: rejected, morose, unappreciated by the public he had selflessly served for decades. "If I were to go over my life again," he confided to his son Thomas, "I would be a shoemaker rather than an American statesman." Not until 1812, after the political enmities had subsided, did Adams and Jefferson renew their old friendship in a series of letters which remain to this day the most remarkable and masterful correspondence in American history.

A recent volume by David Fischer (*The Revolution of American Conservatism,* 1965) presents an entirely different portrait of the Federalist party after 1801. Fischer argues that a second generation of Federalists became politically active after 1801. These younger Federalists, states Fischer, "brought new life to a lost cause, new strength to the shattered enterprises of the old school." Practical men, opportunistically inclined, the younger Federalists, rather than being defeatists, made their peace with democracy and gradually adopted Jeffersonian political principles and practices. Theirs was a double failure, however, according to Fischer: "They failed to find an issue which could carry them to victory, and they failed to erase the destructive stereotype of Federalism which Democrats had stamped upon the minds of the people." Though persuasively argued, Fischer's volume remains unconvincing.

For example, Alexander Hamilton before his death worked tirelessly to reinvigorate the Federalist Party. As early as 1802, when it became apparent that Jefferson's administration was steadily increasing in popularity, Hamilton proposed that some more positive means be utilized to restore the fallen fortunes of his party. Republican victories, according to Hamilton, depended upon a clever trick. By professing to appeal only to the reason of mankind, they were in effect "courting the strongest and the most active passion of the human heart, *vanity!*" Hamilton suggested that the Federalists must copy this technique of cultivating popular favor by addressing themselves to the passions of the voters. "We must renounce our principles and our objects," said Hamilton, "and unite in corrupting public opinion."

Hamilton outlined the platform and organization of an adjunct group to the Federalists, to be called "The Christian Constitutional Society." As the name implied, its tenets were to be support of the Christian religion and the United States Constitution. Members of the society were to contribute five dollars per year. Hamilton detailed its operation: a president and vice-president, a national council of twelve members, statewide subdirecting councils, annual conventions and elections, etc. The society would engage in three types of activity. First, it would foster the formation of correspondence clubs, which would hold weekly meetings and broadcast a steady flow of propaganda. Second, it would, in Hamilton's words, "use . . . all lawful means in *concert* to promote the election of *fit* men." Third, it would promote auxiliary institutions of a "charitable and useful nature." These institutions, for example, by giving relief to immigrants or technical instructions to mechanics, would draw city workers away from "Jacobinism."

Hamilton's lesson plan in the art of practical politics was firmly but tactfully rejected by James A. Bayard of Delaware, Federalist minority leader in Congress. Bayard's reasons are significant, since David Fischer's study uses the Delawarean as an exemplar of the younger Federalist political mentality. Bayard believed Hamilton's proposal would simply duplicate the Republicans' device of regimenting public opinion under the guise of humanitarian motives. This would "revive a thousand jealousies and suspicions which now begin to slumber." Bayard agreed that the Federalists must pay more attention to public opinion. (Virtually every Federalist paid lip service to the necessity of courting the people. Some tried, but the results were disheartening. Wrote Ames in 1803: "Why should I consume my marrow with the fires of that zeal that seems ridiculous to my friends?") "A degree of agitation and vibration of opinion must forever prevail under a government so free as that of the United States," wrote Bayard. "Under such a government, in the nature of things, it is impossible to fix public opinion." The time was not auspicious for Hamilton's scheme. The Federalists must continue "the exertions of good men," as in the past, and wait for that "vibration" which would bring their party back to power. On July 11, 1804, Hamilton was killed by Aaron Burr in a duel fought at Weehauken, New Jersey. Had Hamilton lived it is doubtful that either he or the Christian Constitutional Society could have succeeded in the restoration of Federalism. Almost overnight the party had become a relic, possessed of an antiquated philosophy, a "halfway house," in the words of Henry Adams, "between the European past and the American future."

Only in the Supreme Court, presided over by John Marshall, was the final citadel of Federalism preserved. And Marshall was understandably reluctant to have the court engage in an open political fight with the Republican administration. Such an opportunity presented itself in April, 1802, when the Judiciary Act of 1801 was repealed and Federalist circuit court judges consequently lost their positions. Various Federalist chieftains, including Gouverneur Morris and Roger Griswold, believed the repealing act unconstitutional and wanted the Supreme Court to so declare. But Marshall counseled moderation. In the face of Republican power it would not be wise baldly to challenge them. The law should be obeyed. The following year, under different circumstances, the Supreme Court did declare part of a federal law unconstitutional in the famous case of Marbury v. Madison. But so clever was Marshall's opinion that Jefferson, though opposed to its principles, did nothing publicly to upset the precedent it established. Marshall's brilliance kept the judiciary wedded to Federalism, but in the political arena the minority party was crushed by Republican majorities in virtually every state.

With hopes eroded by despair, and without leaders of national stature, many Northern Federalists inclined toward a radical solution: they sought eventually to separate the Northeastern states from the union. The secessionist group was not constant, and various members flickered in and out of their intrigues. Their geographical center was in the Connecticut valley and their radius of influence extended little further than New England. Among the more important members were Griswold, Jedediah Morse, James Hillhouse, Caleb Strong, William Plumer, and the ringleader of the cabal, the indefatigable Timothy Pickering. They shared a dislike and distrust of Westerners and Southerners, but their special ire was reserved for the "proud" state of Virginia, which they felt had an undue influence in the central government. Since the South would never voluntarily abrogate the three fifths clause of the Constitution, since the Louisiana Purchase assured the continued Southern domination of the federal authority, and since Southern hostility to Northern interests was obvious—so the extremists reasoned—the only alternative was disunion.

The plan was well conceived, but never executed. As outlined by Griswold to Plumer, it contained four logically successive steps. The conspirators would win the state elections in New England and thus gain control of these governments; electoral laws for national congressmen would be repealed, and senators recalled; each state would sever relations with the central government and establish its own collection of customs; ultimately they would combine into a Northern confederation. Not each member of the plot knew all the details. For example, as Lynn Turner has noted, Plumer was unaware that military plans to defend the new confederation had already been charted by the chief conspirators. At the same time, they hoped to carry with them some of the middle Atlantic states, particularly New York. In March, 1804, Oliver Wolcott asked Griswold if New York could be drawn away from the Jeffersonians and freed "from the abhorred domination of the perfidious Virginians." Wolcott was well aware that relations between Jefferson and the Vice President, Aaron Burr, had deteriorated. In fact, the Republican party in New York was split into three factions, represented by the Livingston, Clinton, and Burr groups. None was noted for any devotion to honest means or adherence to principles, but Jefferson clearly allied with the Clinton faction. Moreover, until he was killed in the Weehauken duel, Hamilton led the New York Federalists in sworn opposition to Burr. "Never in the history of the United States," Henry Adams has commented, "did so powerful a combination of rival politicians unite to break down a single man as that which arrayed itself against Burr."

Perhaps with the help of the New England secessionists

Burr could win the gubernatorial race. (So confused were the multiplying rumors, reinforced by great but specious expectations, that some of the plotters believed Burr and Hamilton would cooperate in the disunion movement. The idea of these two "working in double harness," writes Lynn Turner, "was, of course, fantastic.") Before the secessionists would support Burr, however, they wanted to know whether he would pledge himself to disunion, or whether he would use Federalist support as a springboard to the presidency. Burr's reply was characteristically enigmatical and masterfully vague. At a meeting held in Washington with Burr, James Hillhouse carried away the impression that Burr was favorably disposed toward and would cooperate in the formation of a Northern confederacy. Actually, Burr had promised nothing more than a New York administration "satisfactory to the Federalists." Despite this meager response, and despite Hamilton's urgent advice to the contrary, the cabal decided to support Burr. Within a few months Burr was defeated in the elections, and then forced to flee New York as a result of his duel with Hamilton.

Concurrent with these events, the cabal discovered a receptive audience in the person of Anthony Merry, the British minister, who felt it was to England's interest to further secession in America. Merry, however, concluded that the best chance to dismember the American union was not through the creation of a Northern confederacy, but rather by supporting Burr's dream of a Western empire. Merry recommended that the British government subsidize Burr with $500,000 to detach the Western territories from the United States. The money was not advanced but Burr nevertheless proceeded on his ill-fated adventure.

Hamilton had been hostile to the separatist plot. Merry proved sympathetic but refused to participate actively. Moreover, the cabal was unsuccessful in its overtures to Federalist politicians in New Jersey, Pennsylvania, New York, and Delaware. Jefferson, who was apparently informed of the conspiracy, wisely ignored it. But the plot collapsed, fundamentally, because the people of New England were not receptive. After all, commerce prospered under Jefferson's administration. Somehow the churches remained standing. No blood baths took place. The Bank of the United States still operated. Peace was maintained. Every economic indicator continued to rise, undisturbed by Federalist laments of impending anarchy. Lynn Turner, whose account of the conspiracy is definitive, summarized its failure as follows: "Few intrigues have ever fizzled out so ingloriously as the secession plot of 1804, but few plotters have ever built upon so flimsy a foundation. It requires some discontent to arouse a people against their government, and the only dissatisfaction with Jefferson's regime in 1804 existed in the imaginations of the Federalist leaders."

By every index Jefferson's first term as president was an unparalleled success. As John Randolph later recalled: "Never was there an administration more brilliant than that of Mr. Jefferson up to this period. We were indeed in the 'full tide of successful experiment.' Taxes repealed; the public debt amply provided for, both principal and interest; sinecures abolished; Louisiana acquired; public confidence unbounded." The secessionists' vision of a Northern confederacy had collapsed, at least temporarily. The sweeping political victory of the Republican party in 1804 was an expression of public confidence which corroborated Jefferson's faith in the democratic process. (Only a Federalist cynic would think otherwise.) But in the following four years that faith received some severe tests. Jefferson's second term posed renewed problems which bore striking resemblances to those John Adams faced in 1797. War had broken out again between England and France, and once again the United States was forced to walk the tightrope of neutrality. Foreign affairs again took precedence over every other issue, and the question of peace or war again was on every tongue. Like the

Federalist party in 1798-99, the Republicans suffered a schism. From a party which had been spirited and relatively unified in 1801, they broke into quarreling factions.

The most important of the disaffected Republicans was the incomparable but perverse John Randolph, Jr. Yet there is no historical agreement as to when or why the split began. In fact, for more than a century scholars have been fascinated by the problem of explaining the causes of the schism. Some have listed a single significant cause, while others have distinguished between the immediate and fundamental reasons—as if they were discussing a war or revolution. Explanations have run from the personal and psychological make-up of the individuals concerned, through divisions of opinion over specific political events, to theoretical disagreements over basic principles.

For example, several historians believe that an important part of the ill feeling can be traced to the Chase impeachment which Randolph helped to prosecute. Chagrined at his loss, for Chase was acquitted by a combination of Federalist and Republican votes, Randolph may well have concluded that Jefferson had not acted forcefully enough in imposing party discipline. Other writers have stressed Randolph's intense dislike of James Madison. But why this dislike? Again, there is no consensus. Perhaps the alienation began in 1806 when Randolph had solicited the post of minister to Great Britain and was, partly on Secretary of State Madison's advice, rejected by Jefferson. Perhaps Randolph's antagonism commenced much earlier, in his opposition to the settlement by the Jeffersonian administration of the Yazoo land claims. The issue was politically explosive and, in order to find a solution satisfactory to all parties, Jefferson in 1802 appointed a commission composed of Madison, Gallatin, and Levi Lincoln. The commission recommended that purchasers of the Yazoo lands, though their titles were disputable, should "for various equitable considerations," be reimbursed. No one was happy with the specific terms suggested.

The claimants, many of whom were from New England, complained that the compromise was too little, while Georgia protested that not one cent should be paid. Randolph denounced the report in his inimitable style, for sanctioning an "atrocious public robbery." He placed special blame on the figure of Madison and not even Gallatin (for whom Randolph still had some respect) could pacify him. So long as Randolph remained in Congress, and despite pro-administration majorities in that body, he was ever victorious in barring an acceptance of the commission's proposals.

More than one author has suggested that Randolph's hatred for Madison was grounded in jealousy. Randolph aspired to the presidency, yet Madison was the chosen heir. Irving Brant, biographer of Madison, mentions Randolph's personal instability. His voice was high and effeminate; his temper decidedly erratic; his conversation notoriously obscene. Randolph's genital organs, an examining physician reported after his death, were rudimentary. Probably many of his bizarre personal characteristics and much of his warped behavior were compensatory for being sexually underdeveloped.

The mixed bag of causes which scholars have listed for the split would require a thick volume in itself. Apparently the rupture was gradual and, given Randolph's personality, inevitable. Russell Kirk (*Randolph of Roanoke*, 1951), views the division as one involving basic principles. "It was upon this point of rigid construction of the federal compact, this insistence that principles are not to be abandoned no matter how tempting the prospect opened by making exceptions," says Kirk, "that Randolph must have separated from the party of Jefferson even had there been no Yazoo debate, no Florida affair, no embargo; for these issues passed away, and Randolph was not reconciled to the Jeffersonian body." With the single exception of the Louisiana Purchase, which Randolph supported, Kirk maintains that after 1801 Randolph remained steadfastly true to the old Republican doctrines of limited government, strict construction, states' rights, and individual liberty. There were other important differences between the two Virginians. Randolph sneered at Jefferson's natural law beliefs; he rejected Jefferson's equalitarian bent; he had little faith in collective popular reason or majority rule. "I am an aristocrat," said Randolph. "I love liberty, I hate equality." This phrase, writes Kirk, "clearly reveals the gulf between the thought of Jefferson and the thought of Randolph."

One of the strongest links connecting Randolph to Jefferson in the 1790's was their common appreciation of agrarianism. Of course, Randolph's model was the pre-Revolutionary Virginia economy, while Jefferson envisioned a nation mainly of freeholders living in equalitarian simplicity. Both endorsed a natural aristocracy, but Jefferson's was largely self-made and educated, while Randolph's was largely predetermined by family and property. When Jefferson as president appeared to abandon his agrarian leanings; when he purposely invited Northerners into the party and filled key posts with mediocre political hacks from New Jersey, Pennsylvania, and Massachusetts, none of whom had any real commitment to Republican doctrines; when he abandoned strict construction and states' rights; and when he enlarged the executive authority and increased national powers—Randolph felt these evils presaged a new era which he could only deplore.

Most scholars would probably disagree with Kirk's assessment. (See, for example, Bernard Mayo, *Myths and Men,* 1959.) Jefferson was certainly inclined to be introspective and philosophical. Hamilton and John Adams to the contrary, he neither desired nor sought to become a political leader. The dangers to liberty thrust him into that role. As president he applied himself to the business of politics with great diligence, and with no little success. Certainly he was not constant, but above all Jefferson was eminently reasonable. Randolph was really the abstract theorist who lived in a world of illusions. His vision was reactionary, and America continued to progress. Like the Federalists, with whom he later associated in mutual impotency, Randolph was a gloomy critic of democratic growth. He was a man of egocentric single purpose who, rejecting change, found himself outside the mainstream of the developing political system.

Randolph's defection proved not to be a serious threat to the administration. Certainly he and his followers cannot be considered, as John D. Hicks labeled them, the first third party in American history. Even other Republican splinter groups in Pennsylvania and New York did not support Randolph. "Historical evidence," writes Noble Cunningham, "demonstrates the impossibility of connecting Randolph with factions which in state politics were called Quids." The number of "old Republican" congressmen who followed Randolph's lead decreased as the break widened and as Randolph's anti-administration hostility became irreparable. Some scholars have counted approximately twenty Randolph men, including half the Virginia delegation, but this number might have been at the time of the West Florida issue. "The defection of so prominent a leader," Jefferson explained, "threw them into dismay and confusion for a moment." By March, 1806, Jefferson reported that eighty-seven Republicans voted with the administration and only eleven with Randolph. And in May, Jefferson wrote to Monroe: "Upon all trying questions, exclusive of the federalists, the minority of republicans voting with him has been from 4 to 6 or 8, against from 90 to 100."

Two years later a more serious division took place in the ranks of Republicanism, over the choice of a presidential candidate. James Madison was Jefferson's obvious favorite, and by all standards Madison deserved the nomination. But many Republicans, for different reasons, considered Madison weak and inept, and preferred James Monroe. Randolph then wrote, and sixteen of his cohorts signed, an uncompromising protest against the decision of the congressional caucus selecting Madison: "We ask for energy, and we are told of his moderation. We ask for talents, and the reply is his unassuming merit. We ask what were his services in the cause of public liberty, and we are directed to the pages of the *Federalist,* written in conjunction with Alexander Hamilton and John Jay, in which the most extravagant of their doctrines are maintained and propagated. We ask for consistency as a Republican, standing forth to stem the torrent of oppression which once threatened to overwhelm the liberties of the country. We ask for that high and honorable sense of duty which would at all times turn with loathing and abhorrence from any compromise with fraud and speculation. We ask in vain." However, Monroe's supporters did not come, in the main, from Randolph's "old Republicans." In fact, Monroe was cautioned by several of his Virginia associates, writes Noble Cunningham, "that he would have no chance if he appeared to be an anti-administration candidate."

Monroe was not the only politician who thought of sitting in the chair Jefferson was about to vacate. Vice-President George Clinton, feeble and bordering on senility, was put forward as an anti-embargo presidential candidate from New York. Many Federalists hoped to coalesce the forces opposed to the embargo, unite behind Clinton, and in one supreme effort overthrow the Jefferson-Madison machine. But the Federalist alliance with Clinton failed to materialize. For Clinton again received the national Republican nomination for Vice President, to be ticketed with Madison, and he accepted. Federalist politicians from eight states, meeting in New York, had to content themselves with nominating their stalwarts Charles C. Pinckney and Rufus King. The results of the election reveal the immense popular support of the Republican administration. Outside New England, Madison swept most of the country, receiving 122 electoral votes to Pinckney's 47, while Clinton gained 6, all of which were from New York. In Virginia, Madison triumphed over Monroe by more than a four-to-one margin. This "disastrous defeat," according to Norman K. Risjord (*The Old Republicans*, 1965), ". . . precluded the formation of a Southern-oriented third party." Republican power in the lower House decreased, but they still enjoyed an impressive majority of forty-six over the Federalists.

Jefferson's joy at the prospect of retiring to Monticello was boundless. He was bone-weary. Yet he had preserved his party. The secessionist plots of Federalist extremists had been aborted. The Republican party schisms remained a minor irritant which Jefferson, through wise leadership, never permitted to spread. The accomplishments of the Federalist era resulted from complementary achievement, the clash of principles between emerging parties. But the accomplishments of the Jeffersonian era resulted from the dominance of a single party, which was in turn dominated by a single man. The retirement of Jefferson marked the beginning of the disintegration of the Republicans.

JEFFERSON KEEPS THE PEACE

"We have no alternative but to keep the balance between an appeasement which would betray us by weakness and a brinkmanship which would destroy us by miscalculation." The words were those of Adlai Stevenson in 1964, but they could well serve to describe America's problem in foreign relations during the administrations of Jefferson and Madison. For nearly a decade, but especially after 1806, war fevers mounted ominously and then subsided cautiously, only to spiral suddenly upwards and then abate once again. "The question of peace or war," wrote George Clinton in 1807, "is as difficult to answer as ever." In 1808 Thomas Tucker told John Page: "I can scarcely give you an opinion on the subject of peace or war." Shortly after his retirement in 1809, Jefferson admitted: "How long we may yet retain . . . [peace] is difficult to be foreseen."

Ever since war between England and France was renewed, the United States had sought a policy which would steer a neutral course between the two great powers, which would convince them to respect American sovereign rights on the high seas, which would not commit the country to an open conflict, and which would be acceptable to the majority of American citizens. A policy meeting all these conditions was never found, and eventually the United States declared war on England. But it is curious and revealing that many contemporaries—and some of today's scholars—who criticized Jefferson's course as one of bumbling and humiliating appeasement also condemn Madison's diplomatic mismanagement that finally led him to ask Congress for war. One is tempted to paraphrase Page Smith's remark on the Alien and Sedition Acts: We can leave the harsh criticisms of Republican foreign policy to the infallible historians, who will be happy if their own nations and their own times can provide any better solutions for maintaining the peace.

In 1806, through pressure from Congress, Jefferson dispatched William Pinkney to join the American ambassador, James Monroe, in London. Their instructions were to secure from Britain an abandonment of the practice of impressment and resumption of the right of "broken voyages." If these were not admitted the United States would impose a retaliatory act prohibiting the importation of certain English products. Britain did make some allowances in the West Indian trade, and even signed a diplomatic note assuring the United States that they would try to avoid impressing *bona fide* Americans. However, they refused to include any concession on impressment in the formal treaty. Moreover, at the last moment the British attached two significant provisions. One insultingly referred to "the foolish and teasing measure of non-importation" and specified that for ten years the United States must promise not to employ any measures of economic coercion against England. The second, a note annexed to the treaty, reserved to Great Britain the privilege of non-ratification if the United States did not take positive measures against Napoleon's recently enacted Berlin decree. Despite these provisions, and in violation of their instructions, Pinkney and Monroe signed the treaty.

Jefferson decided to reject the treaty, and it was never submitted to the Senate. But its contents eventually became common knowledge. Federalists and some anti-administration Republicans belabored what they mistakenly believed to be Jefferson's duplicity. "Your President," said James Bayard, "never meant to have a treaty with Great Britain. If he had intended it, he would never have fettered the commissioners with *sine qua non*'s which were insuperable." Monroe was so chagrined that he responded to Randolph's overtures and allowed his name to be placed in opposition to Madison's in the 1808 presidential race. Some scholars have echoed the criticisms of Jefferson's decision. "He threw away an irreplaceable instrument for stilling the growing strife between the two countries," states A. L. Burt (*The United States, Great Britain, and British North America,* 1940), "and he also contributed to the increase of this strife." Bradford Perkins (*Prologue to War: England and the United States,* 1961), feels that, given the relative strength of England and the United States, the French threat, and the benefits that would have accrued to American commerce, Monroe and Pinkney were "justified" in signing the treaty. Monroe and Pinkney, he writes, "spoke the traditional accents of American realism" in opposition to Madison's and Jefferson's well-intentioned but misplaced idealism.

Perhaps. Much of this is hindsight wisdom. In fair rebuttal, as Perkins admits, the treaty would have deprived the United States of the only real economic weapon she possessed. Moreover, it would have allied the United States with Britain against France, a course contrary to Republican diplomatic tenets. After all, the effects of Jay's Treaty a decade earlier led to American involvement in an undeclared naval war with

France, and Jefferson had always remained dubious of the treaty's value. Why repeat the dismal history of that decade? It was still possible to find a peaceful settlement with both nations without being intimidated by either one into an entangling alliance. The instrument Jefferson was eager to use, the penultimate policy, was full-scale economic coercion by a total embargo.

However in June, 1807, a flagrant act took place which threatened to sweep away other alternatives. A British man-of-war, H.M.S. *Leopard,* fired three broadsides at close range into the side of the American frigate *Chesapeake.* The stricken vessel was boarded by a British search party, and four alleged deserters were removed. Only one was beyond doubt a British subject. After the *Chesapeake* limped back to Norfolk, carrying twenty-one dead or wounded, war fever swept the United States. "Never, since the battle of Lexington," Jefferson wrote to Lafayette, "have I seen this country in such a state of exasperation as at present. And even that did not produce such unanimity." Naturally, Jefferson demanded satisfaction. England was to disavow the act, grant reparations, recall the offending Admiral Berkeley, and return the men taken from the *Chesapeake.* Even more, Jefferson again insisted that Great Britain discontinue the practice of impressment. Monroe was instructed by Madison that "as a security for the future, an entire abolition of impressments from vessels under the flag of the United States . . . is . . . to make an indispensable part of the satisfaction."

Historians agree that Jefferson erred in coupling the two demands, but Henry Adams's evaluation of Jefferson's behavior is more severe. The United States, wrote Adams, "hesitated to fight when a foreign nation, after robbing their commerce, fired into their ships of sea, and slaughtered or carried off their fellow citizens. . . . Jefferson and his government had shown over and over again that no provocation would make them fight; and from the moment this attitude was understood, America became fair prey." Bradford Perkins thinks that Jefferson's chief mistake consisted of missing the peak psychological moment of offended patriotism which united the nation against England. His temporizing attitude permitted the erosion of sentiment for war. Later, says Perkins, Jefferson tried to restore the demand for war, and made several bellicose gestures. "But the popular spirit had evaporated, the orators had fallen silent," writes Perkins. Even if Jefferson changed his mind (Perkins thinks this probable) it was too late.

These criticisms contain a degree of validity. It is difficult to say when a government, with legitimate grievances, with substantial grounds for war, should cease a policy of peace. If one assumes that war is inevitable, then a wise government should choose the most propitious moment. One must also agree with Henry Adams that constant appeasement invites insult and aggression. Without a doubt the unity of 1807 would have made it a preferable time to 1812, when war was declared against the will of a substantial minority of the American people. Similarly, most scholars reviewing the fundamental causes of the Second World War, condemn Neville Chamberlain's appeasement at Munich. But to Thomas Jefferson war was not inevitable. It represented the last resort of diplomatic bankruptcy, an escape from the admittedly difficult problems which the United States faced as the world's leading neutral carrier. As Dexter Perkins has commented (*The American Approach to Foreign Policy,* 1952), "the idealism of Jefferson played no small part in the development of the American mind. And war runs counter to any such point of view." Jefferson tried to use the threat of war as a diplomatic weapon many times, and each bluster was less effective. The point Henry Adams missed, however, is that Jefferson could but profit from a war, politically and personally, and a lesser man would have capitalized upon the passions of an aroused nationalism. Many disaffected Republicans, such as Randolph, favored a policy of immediate retaliation. Even most Federalists, immediately after the *Chesapeake* affair, would have admitted the complete justification of war.

But Jefferson chose the embargo rather than war. The act prohibited virtually all exports from the United States. Vessels engaged in fishing or coastal trade were permitted to continue their operations, but were required to post bonds that their cargoes were destined for a United States port. The effect upon the American economy was catastrophic: idle ships, bankruptcies, unemployment, falling prices, even a few suicides. The Federalist party in New England was rejuvenated, and new secessionist plots were hatched. After a fifteen month trial the embargo was repealed. The most dramatic act of Jefferson's second administration proved an unpopular and costly failure.

The embargo, then and now, has been an easy mark for denunciation. Much has been written about its relative effects upon England and the United States. The undeniable conclusion is that England suffered less than the United States, and France appeared to be indifferent to it. The Lancashire mills ran short of cotton, the West Indies of food, and the Irish linen industry of flax. But in general the embargo did not seriously disrupt the British economy. Even the sale of British manufactured goods found new outlets in South American nations, then in rebellion against Spain, to take up the slack in American purchases. "Would to God," thundered one Federalist, "that the Embargo had done as little evil to ourselves as it has done to foreign nations." American agriculture suffered a sharp decrease in prices, but the shrillest complaints emanated from the Northern commercial centers.

Jefferson knew that the embargo required a considerable sacrifice upon the part of the American people. But his error was twofold. He badly overestimated the dependence of the British economy on the United States, and he relied too heavily upon the cooperation of Americans. Rather than cooperate, the North openly defied the embargo. "Let every man who holds the name of America dear to him," declared a typical Massachusetts circular, "stretch forth his hands and put this accursed thing, this *Embargo* from him." Smuggling of goods across the Canadian border became a major enterprise, and the lawbreakers suffered no qualms of disloyalty. Jefferson had been mistaken, writes Bradford Perkins, in asking for "superhuman self-denial from a nation that had perhaps been corrupted by prosperity."

The loopholes in the original legislation, the smuggling, the cynical lack of cooperation by governors and other state officials in New England, forced the Republican administration to pass supplemental acts to strengthen the enforcement of the embargo. Thus it became, as one historian has concluded: "The most arbitrary, inquisitorial, and confiscatory measure formulated in American legislation up to the period of the Civil War." Nathan Schachner (*Thomas Jefferson,* 1951), agrees that the embargo "clamped on states and private citizens a series of controls, restrictions and regulations for which little justification could be found in the express terms of the Constitution." True enough, but the fact remains that these acts of desperation were caused by the constant violations and the open defiance of New England. Jefferson was fighting an internal conflict with the Northern Federalists in order to avoid war with England. (Abraham Lincoln took stronger measures to control the Copperheads in an analogous case.) The Northern Federalists "are endeavoring to convince England that we suffer more by the Embargo than they do," wrote Jefferson in June, 1808, "and if they will but hold out a while, we must abandon it. . . . But if this is before the repeal of the orders in council, we must abandon it only for a state of war."

However one interprets the basic purpose of the embargo, Jefferson cannot escape scholarly disapproval. On the one hand the embargo was a weapon of coercion, designed to force British and French recognition of America's neutral rights. "Such a stickling for the extreme of [neutral rights], such an irritation constantly kept up," wrote Richard Hildreth more than a century ago, "must lead inevitably to war, the Federalists had foreseen from the beginning." On the other hand, by keeping American ships at home, the embargo can also be considered as a surrender and abdication of neutral rights. In direct contradiction to Hildreth, authors Robert G. Albion and Jennie B. Pope (*Sea Lanes in Wartime,* 1942), regard the embargo as "the negation of freedom of the seas." Finally, Bradford Perkins's study contains a thorough condemnation of the embargo. It failed as coercion; it delayed war but failed to keep the peace; it destroyed American unity and wounded the American economy; it evoked Federalist extremism; it humiliated America in European capitals; and, writes Perkins, "it provided an excuse for ineffective military preparations when force was the only language the world understood."

This fundamental assumption—that force was the only language the world understood—is precisely the philosophy that Jefferson resisted. And his followers to this day hold, mistakenly or not, that it must be resisted.

THE WAR OF 1812

The figure of James Madison calls up the sarcasm of Washington Irving's comment in 1811: "Poor Jemmy! He is but a withered little apple-John." Madison's administration was one of irresolution and indirection; a rudderless ship, mutinous mates, tossed about in a storm which blew across from Europe. Actually a warmer individual than Jefferson, he could not project an engaging image. Somehow Madison appears drab, especially when contrasted with the new personalities in Washington such as the aggressive Henry Clay and the incisive John C. Calhoun.

"Always hoping for harmony," writes William N. Chambers, "he proved reluctant to fight, surprisingly inept in handling appointments and patronage to strengthen party cohesion. . . . Once an able Congressional party leader, he seemed increasingly lost in the problems of party as he became more and more absorbed in the trying problems of state." Contrast, for example, the political dexterity of Jefferson in dealing with the ambitious Smith brothers of Maryland, the unpredictable William Branch Giles, the New York Clintonians, or the anti-Gallatin Republicans of Pennsylvania. All bordered on the schismatic, at one time or another, but Jefferson adroitly kept them loyal to his administration. Madison did not. These groups opposed the choice of Albert Gallatin as Secretary of State and Madison succumbed to their pressures. He appointed Robert Smith, who had already displayed his utter incompetency as Jefferson's Secretary of the Navy. Madison had hoped to avoid an intra-party struggle, but the appointment boded ill for the Republican future. Other congressmen assumed that Madison was weak, vacillating, and easily dominated. Since Gallatin stayed on as Secretary of the Treasury, cabinet conflicts raged. Smith proved to be mediocre at best, even disloyal to Madison, and in two years he was replaced by James Monroe. Naturally, the removal did not endear Madison to the Smith clique.

Madison had many requisites as Jefferson's heir to the presidency—honesty, experience, dedication, intelligence—but he was not a leader. Even Irving Brant's multivolume appreciation cannot persuade historians that Madison was a great president. His friendship with Jefferson continued after 1809 but, says Bradford Perkins, "he seldom sought Jefferson's advice. Madison's mistakes were his own."

War did not follow upon the abandonment of the embargo. Rather, a compromise piece of legislation, the Nonintercourse Act, took its place. By this law no imports or exports were permitted with England or France, or their respective empires, nor could their armed ships enter an American port. However, nonintercourse toward either country was revokable at the President's initiative if the Decrees or Orders in Council were abrogated. The act was little more than a face-saving device which put a premium on dishonesty. Once an American ship left port it could go anywhere, and Great Britain was usually its destination. But three months later the American people were astounded to hear that the British had capitulated. "Great and Glorious News," declared the New Hampshire *Patriot,* "Our Differences with Great Britain Amicably Settled." The whole nation was jubilant. Republicans rejoiced that their system had worked; Federalists rejoiced that their opposition had forced Madison to a policy of reconciliation. "Probably no other event from 1783 to 1815 was so generally celebrated" as the Erskine Agreement, Bradford Perkins writes.

David Erskine, the young British Minister to the United States, had violated George Canning's instructions. Like Monroe and Pinkney three years earlier, Erskine had been provided with *sine qua non*'s which were to be included before a settlement could be arranged. Like them, eager to conclude an agreement, he followed the spirit (so he thought) rather than the letter of his orders. As Monroe and Pinkney's treaty had been disavowed by Jefferson, so Canning repudiated Erskine's. Unfortunately for the United States, Madison had not waited for Canning's reaction. He ordered trade open with England, and hundreds of American ships loaded with raw materials raced across the Atlantic. The cumulative effects of the Embargo and Nonintercourse acts had begun to pinch the British, and the incoming cargoes relieved the economic pressures.

Madison was crestfallen. Erskine was replaced by the officious and insulting "Copenhagen" Jackson. Relations with England worsened. Napoleon continued his policy of insult. Republican spokesmen in Congress quarreled. Executive leadership was practically nonexistent. Federalist gains seemed ominous. "The spirit of the nation is evaporated," said William Burwell, "and I despair of taking any measure . . . which would not meet with such opposition as to make it useless." Finally, after a period of drift and indecision, Congress on May 1, 1810, admitted the failure of economic coercion by passing Macon's Bill No. 2, reopening trade with England and France without any restrictions. The basis of the bill was bribery, which might bring peace or force the issue of war to a head: if either England or France repealed its laws which violated neutral rights, then the United States would impose commercial restrictions upon the other. Madison was less than pleased with the efficacy of this legislation. But he predicted that since the bill benefited England, perhaps Napoleon might reverse his policy.

Napoleon was indeed prodded to take advantage of Macon's Bill No. 2. He instructed his foreign minister, the Duke of Cadore, to inform the American minister that the Berlin and Milan decrees would be removed after November 1, 1810, if in the interim England did the same or if in the interim the United States restored commercial prohibitions against England. Certain phrases in Cadore's letter sent to the American minister were edited by Napoleon, and were purposely equivocal. Macon's Bill did not anticipate preconditions. In fact, the bill cautioned the President that convincing proof of repeal was necessary. But again Madison acted precipitately, with no proof of Napoleon's sincerity, and with serious risks for America. In short, he took Napoleon's bait. By presidential proclamation Madison announced that the edicts of France had been revoked, and England was given three months to suspend the Orders in Council or nonintercourse with the United States would be reimposed.

In the next twenty months, from the time of Madison's proclamation to the American declaration of war, Napoleon's duplicity could hardly be ignored. By the Trianon decree American ships and cargoes, previously sequestered, were auctioned off and the proceeds placed in the French treasury. French hostility to American commerce increased after the Cadore letter. Even a Republican editor admitted France's bad faith, but "the question is not which nation alone is culpable, as they are both so: The only question is, which is the *greatest* and most *iniquitous* aggressor?" Nathaniel Macon declared "the Devil himself could not tell which government, England or France, is the most wicked." England did not lift her Orders in Council for it seemed obvious that Napoleon's decrees were still being enforced. Nevertheless, Madison persisted unreasonably, unfairly, and dangerously, according to some historians, upon the application of commercial restrictions against England. "Perhaps," suggests Bradford Perkins, "in part because he had suffered such deep humiliation through the Erskine agreement, James Madison refused to admit that he had erred."

Yet, as Roger Brown (*Republic in Peril,* 1964) and Irving Brant make clear, Madison was his own man. He understood that Napoleon's technical renunciation of the decrees was an exercise in duplicity. "At no time was Madison deceived by an imperial system under which American vessels were burned at sea instead of being captured under French decrees," writes Brant. "But, the decrees being technically revoked, it suited the legal basis of the President's position toward Britain to treat them in that light." Moreover, Madison did not seek war to escape humiliation. He did not drift into war. He was not intimidated into war by the War Hawks. Even when Gallatin changed his mind and advised that war was avoidable and non-importation should be continued, Madison remained firm. Every inducement, threat, appeal, or concession had been repudiated by Great Britain. No other policy remained after negotiations with the British Minister, Augustus Foster, had collapsed. Thus, Madison had acted responsibly, correctly, even courageously. "One sure way of avoiding war in 1812," writes Roger Brown, "was to abandon the effort to protect American commerce against the Orders of Council. Opposition leaders, John Randolph of Roanoke and some Federalists, advocated this course. Jefferson and Madison believed this to be impossible, economically, morally, and above all, politically."

If Madison led the nation into the War of 1812, rightly or wrongly, he could not have done so without congressional and popular support. These individuals and groups had motives, expressed or secret, rationalized or confused, real or fancied, political or personal, economic or historical, and from this complexity of motives the scholar has sought the most pervasive and fundamental causes for war. Nineteenth century historians, whether pro- or anti-Republican, concurred with the official explanation presented by Madison, that the War of 1812 was brought about by violations of American maritime rights. Various twentieth century scholars, on the other hand, have long debated the reasons for and extent of Western and Southern involvement in the American decision for war.

A breakdown of congressional balloting confirms that most Southerners and Westerners voted affirmatively, while a majority of New Englanders voted negatively. One Boston newspaper complained: "We, whose soil was the hotbed and whose ships were the nursery of Sailors, are insulted with the hypocrisy of a devotedness to Sailors' rights, and the arrogance of a pretended skill in maritime jurisprudence, by those whose country furnishes no navigation beyond the size of a ferryboat or an Indian canoe." The apparent incongruity of a war for maritime rights brought about by the West has intrigued scholars, but there is little accord on exactly why the West wanted war, or even if the Western role was decisive. Every thesis presented has evoked rebuttals and counterclaims. (1) More than forty years ago Louis Hacker "conjectured" that Westerners supported war in order to win the rich farm lands of Canada. Julius Pratt dissented. Abundant land, cheap and fertile, wrote

Pratt, remained unoccupied on the American side of the boundary. (2) Pratt's own thesis stressed a bargain between Northwestern frontiersmen who wanted Canada added to the union, and Southerners who wanted Florida incorporated. A. L. Burt and others rejected Pratt's claim for its lack of empirical evidence. (3) Pratt argued that Westerners desired Canada as part of their natural expansionist tendencies. Reginald Horsman (*The Causes of the War of 1812,* 1962) has concluded that Canada represented to Westerners the center of British incitement of the Indians and an available war target: "The conquest of Canada was primarily a means of waging war, not a reason for starting it." (4) George Taylor and Margaret Latimer, in separate essays, point out that Westerners and Southerners suffered a recession starting in 1808. Inhabitants of these sections blamed England's Orders in Council for their restricted markets and falling prices, and therefore advocated war as an economic panacea. An article by Norman Risjord repudiates by indirection the logic of the Taylor-Latimer thesis. Farmers in the middle-Atlantic states enjoyed prosperity during the same period, Risjord maintains, yet their representatives also advocated war. (5) Many historians today accept "American nationalism" as "the primary factor responsible for the war," writes Risjord. The concept is at once vague and comprehensive enough to embrace all conflicting opinions. Even scholars who subscribe to it disagree. Horsman, for example, finds the fundamental cause of the war in "British maritime policy which hurt both national pride and the commerce of the United States." (Harry Coles, *The War of 1812,* 1965). Yet Horsman insists that a small but earnest group of Republican congressmen (twenty-eight in number, mainly from the West and South) were determined to bring the United States into war. These War Hawks, led by Speaker of the House Henry Clay, succeeded in persuading a majority to vote with them. Roger Brown questions the propriety of the term "War Hawks." The decision for war, according to Brown, was the work of Republicans from every section of the country who believed that national honor and the tenets of their party were at stake.

If the student is perplexed when confronted with this welter of contradictory interpretation, he should bear in mind the advice of Paul Varg (*Foreign Policies of the Founding Fathers,* 1963). Attempting to establish a priority of causes for the War of 1812—or most major wars, for that matter—"leads to a kind of mechanistic conception of social causation that is inconsistent with the very nature of society and of human motivation." Westerners who desired war did so for many reasons, and who can tell which was paramount? They were disturbed by British insults to the American flag and thought it was time to fight since negotiations had failed. They were convinced that the British were responsible for the Indian war on the Wabash. They wanted the British monopoly of the fur trade broken. They blamed Britain for low prices and hard times. They never doubted that some day the American flag would fly over Canada. Even Madison said, referring to Canada: "When the pear is ripe, it will fall of itself." Expansionism accurately describes the sentiment of Westerners from the pre-Revolutionary period to the Civil War, a movement as inexorable as a flow of lava. Surely some Westerners dreamed of ousting Great Britain from the North American continent by possessing Canada. Thus the conquest of Canada seemed a natural object of the war. The day Madison signed the declaration of war, Henry Clay explained why Congress did not elect to fight France at the same time: "The one we can strike, the other we cannot reach."

In Congress the Western and Southern War Hawks, though in the minority, were the activists who pushed and persuaded others to war. They represented a new spirit in Republicanism, and a new force in the nation. The aggressive Young Republicans came to dominate the lower House—establishing Clay as speaker, controlling the caucuses, furthering the system of standing committees. It was Clay who, after consulting with Secretary of State Monroe, suggested a thirty day embargo to be followed by war. It was Calhoun who helped draft the final war message and introduced the resolution for war on June 1st. Even in the Senate the War Hawks, as Randolph sarcastically named them, were not without influence. "All told," says William Chambers, "the policies of the Young Republicans gave their forest-fire faction great resources of power."

But it does not follow that these congressional War Hawks wanted war to gain Canada. A close reading of Clay's public speeches and private letters reveals that he rarely referred to Western expansionism in connection with the war. In fact, he did not espouse war before the autumn of 1811. And when he did, the themes he emphasized were British impressment of sailors and confiscation of ships, and British responsibility for Indian raids on American settlers. When Randolph chided him by asking what *new* causes for war existed, Clay was forced to admit that war should have been declared when Jefferson's embargo was withdrawn. "Those who voted for the former embargo," concluded Clay, "are bound now to vote for war." The War Hawks could not have induced their Northeastern Republican brethren to vote for war if they were not already inducible. Ideologically the reasons that Northerners voted for war were comparable to those listed by Clay and Madison. Eighteen Republicans from the Northeast broke party ranks and voted against the war, yet forty Republicans from the same region voted affirmatively. On a strictly numerical basis the Republican vote for war followed party rather than geographic lines, as Roger Brown claims. But the dominating drive for conflict originated and was furthered in the main by the War Hawks. In that respect it was sectionally inspired, as Reginald Horsman maintains.

A few months before the declaration of war, some Federalists had boasted that they would welcome a conflict, for it would destroy the Republican administration. The Federalists would then come into power and arrange a peace with England. But by June they felt otherwise, and offered their traditional arguments for continued neutrality. Madison might deny it, was their main theme, but by warring against England the United States would become the ally of France. "We are about to make common cause with a man," stated one Federalist, "who hates us for our language and despises us for our government, and who would tomorrow, if he had the means, add us to the list of his conquered provinces." Moreover, the United States was unprepared. Time was needed—time to recruit, train, and arm men, to garrison seaboard and frontier, to build a strong army and navy. Most important, the Federalists lingered on the economic sacrifice war would entail. Trade amounting to thirty-five million dollars a year with Great Britain would be lost. The American merchant marine would be swept off the seas. Commerce would be decimated. Federalists pled for a policy of protraction. Some promised to support an embargo for six months—anything but war. It was too late. They had had their chance. They had crippled the embargo by evasion. Now their pleas were futile.

The New England Federalists never supported the War of 1812 and from its inception the country was troubled by the possibility of secession. William Plumer, an ex-Federalist who had been party to the conspiracy of 1804 and knew full well the temper of the extremists, did not doubt that separation was contemplated. James Bayard, the Federalist member of the bi-partisan mission sent to Russia when that country offered to mediate between England and the United States, accepted the commission because "the situation of public affairs is at present . . . critical and alarming, not from the pressure of the foreign enemy, but from the danger of intestine division." New Eng-landers supplied enemy forces with food. When Albert Gallatin asked for subscriptions to war loans, Boston financiers refused.

Federalist governors openly defied Madison and would not permit their militia to fight outside state boundaries. Northern newspapers freely printed inflammatory articles which were disloyal if not treasonous. All this was fully reported in England, providing an erroneous conception of American opinion, and convincing the British to persevere in the war. No wonder Madison "looks miserably shattered and woe-begone," William Wirt wrote. "His mind is full of the New England sedition."

The New England secession movement of 1814-15 was not a conspiracy of disgruntled politicians. It was a popular movement, first stirred by the embargo and catalyzed by the war. Federalist leaders cultivated the discontent and reaped the rewards. In 1814 they swept the elections. Timothy Pickering was again at the center of disunionist activities, zealous as ever. Finally the Massachusetts legislature issued a call for a convention "to lay the foundation for a radical reform in the National compact." Were they to advocate secession, the people were undoubtedly ready to accept the decision. President Madison became sufficiently alarmed, albeit belatedly, to prepare plans "to repel the enemy and put rebellion down."

The Hartford Convention was controlled by moderates from the outset. Except for Pickering, the few remaining members of the Essex Junto opposed secession. "The worst of all evils," said George Cabot, head of the Massachusetts delegation, "would be a dissolution of the Union." Other Federalists, such as Harrison G. Otis, shared this sentiment. Instead of secession they passed a series of proposals for constitutional amendments: abrogation of the three fifths clause; office holding to be confined to the native born; a one term limit for the presidency; a two thirds vote of Congress to admit new states, or to pass legislation restricting commerce, or to declare war.

Even while the convention was in session, from December 15, 1814, to January 5, 1815, public attention shifted from Hartford to New Orleans. British troops, led by the brother-in-

law of the Duke of Wellington, Major General Edward Paken-
ham, were beginning to close in on the city. His 8,000 men
were veterans, including those who had captured and burned
the capital. Facing them were a motley mixture of Kentucky
and Tennessee militiamen, a few regulars, riverboatmen, smug-
glers, freed Negroes, and French Louisianans, commanded by
Andrew Jackson. The Federalist papers predicted a British victory. Timothy Pickering gloated that the union would be severed.
The British would accomplish what the Hartford Convention
had not.

News of Jackson's astonishing victory, and hard on its
heels, news from Ghent of the peace treaty with England,
stunned the Federalists. The Hartford Convention had assigned
three delegates to present its resolutions to the national government. "Their position," commented the French minister, Louis
Sérurier, "was awkward, embarrassing, and lent itself cruelly
to ridicule." Two of the Federalists paid their respects to Madison but left without performing their mission. Republicans everywhere, but particularly in New England where they had been
suppressed by hostile public opinion, joyously celebrated and
acclaimed Madison for his "perseverance in a season of dark-
ness and difficulty."

A proud glow of nationalism suffused the American people, especially when they recollected how early defeats were
weathered and the final victory was theirs. Washington had been
burned, but on the ocean the Americans had won two of every
three fights. And Jackson's victory at New Orleans was incomparable! Only seven Americans were killed and six wounded,
while the British counted 700 killed, 1400 wounded, and 500
captured. Mighty and haughty Britain had conquered Napoleon
but could not conquer America. Even the peace treaty, which
provided for a territorial settlement based on *status quo ante
bellum,* was regarded as an American triumph. "The war has
given the Americans what they so essentially lacked," wrote

Sérurier, "a national character founded on a glory common to all."

Only a quarter of a century had passed since the ratification of the Constitution launched a new nation, and it had survived authoritarian impulses, secessionist plots, political alarms, and British arms. The "withered little apple-John," by a combination of fortune and fortitude, had steered the American people from near disaster to a new era of national self-respect. With a free and open land stretching to the Rockies, with a commercial potential destined to rule the oceans, with a solid peace and flourishing economy, with a vigorous and harmonious people in the full possession of liberty, no one in 1815 could doubt the American future. The party Madison had formed and then co-directed with Jefferson was now the obvious party of that future. Victory had cured its major schisms as it had depressed the Federalists. "A glorious opportunity" presented itself, wrote Joseph Story, "for the Republican party to place themselves permanently in power."

So it seemed.

Selected Bibliography

The best biography of George Washington is the multivolume study written by his fellow Virginian, Douglas Southall Freeman, *George Washington: A Biography* (7 vols., New York, 1948-57). It is massive and detailed rather than interpretive. Typically, Freeman keeps the focus on the central figure, whom he admires but does not adulate. The last volume, completed after his death, was written by John A. Carroll and Mary W. Ashworth. Carroll's evaluation of Washington as president is contained in Morton Borden (ed.), *America's Ten Greatest Presidents* (Chicago, 1961). A clever volume of Washington and his legend, useful as a supplement to Freeman, is Marcus Cunliffe, *George Washington: Man and Monument* (Boston, 1958). No great biography of Hamilton exists. One of the most recent by Broadus Mitchell, *Alexander Hamilton* (2 vols., New York, 1957-62) is marred by an anti-Jeffersonian bias. A better treatment, but uninspired, is by John C. Miller, *Alexander Hamilton, Portrait in Paradox* (New York, 1959). Irving Brant's multivolume study, *James Madison* (6 vols., Indianapolis, 1948-61) sparked a "Madisonian revival" which, if accepted, would make him a greater figure than Jefferson. The definitive study of Jefferson, but yet uncompleted, is by Dumas Malone, *Jefferson and His Time* (3 vols., Boston, 1948-62). A shorter work by Nathan Schachner, *Thomas Jefferson: A Biography* (2 vols., New York, 1951) is acceptable but mundane. Leonard Levy, *Jefferson and Civil Liberties: The Darker Side* (Cambridge, 1963) presents an iconoclastic view of Jefferson's alleged libertarianism. Page Smith's recent *John Adams* (2 vols., New York, 1962) has won critical and popular acclaim. His study depends heavily—almost exclusively—on the Adams papers. It supplants the older but still useful study of Gilbert Chinard, *Honest John Adams* (Boston, 1933). Stephen Kurtz's *The Presidency of John Adams* (Philadelphia, 1957) devotes much attention to the conflict over and aftermath of the Jay treaty. The figure of James Monroe has yet to find a superior biographer, but perhaps the problem rests with the subject. John Taylor also needs a competent, full-length treatment, for Henry Simms, *Life of John Taylor* (Richmond, 1932) is woefully inadequate. Henry Adams's old study, *The Life of Albert Gallatin* (Philadelphia, 1879) is unwieldy and the reader is directed to the more recent work by Raymond Walters, Jr., *Albert Gallatin: Jeffersonian Financier and Diplomat* (New York, 1957). For an appreciation of the Federalist position, Lynn Turner's *William Plumer of New Hampshire* (Chapel Hill, 1962) is a model biography. Also useful are Samuel E. Morison, *The Life and Letters of Harrison Gray Otis* (2 vols., Boston, 1913); Morton Borden *The Federalism of James A. Bayard* (New York, 1955); and Winfred Bernhard, *Fisher Ames: Federalist and Statesman* (Chapel Hill, 1965). Russell Kirk's work, *Randolph of Roanoke* (Chicago, 1951) is not a biography, but a *tour de force,* indispensable for anyone who wishes to understand Barry Goldwater. Albert Beveridge, *The Life of John Marshall* (4 vols., Boston, 1916-19) reveals as much about Beveridge as it does about Marshall. Burr remains an enigma but a good introduction to him has been done by Nathan Schachner, *Aaron Burr* (New York, 1937).

Some works covering the early national period should be avoided. The studies of Claude Bowers, *Jefferson and Hamilton: The Struggle for Democracy in America* (Boston, 1925) and *Jefferson in Power: The Death Struggle of the Federalists* (Boston, 1936) are journalistic and slanted against the Federalists. Students generally enjoy reading Bowers for his color and fast pace, but the volumes contain innumerable errors of fact and dubious interpretations. John Dos Passos's *The Men Who Made the Nation* (New York, 1957) is unacceptable. Nathan Schachner's *The Founding Fathers* (New York, 1954) is long-winded but competent. A suggestive survey of the period 1789-1837, in impeccable style, and highly recommended, is Marcus Cunliffe's *The Nation Takes Shape* (Chicago, 1959). Charles Wiltse, *The New Nation, 1800-1845* (New York, 1961) is perhaps less revisionist than claimed. William N. Chambers, *Political Parties in a New Nation: The American Experience, 1776-1809* (New York, 1963) is the work of a political scientist applying the knowledge of his discipline to history, with happy results. Seymour Lipset, *The First New Nation: The United States in Historical and Comparative Perspective* (New York, 1963) is the work of a sociologist applying the tools of his discipline to the same subject, with less fortunate results. It is instructive to contrast how this volume was reviewed by professional sociologists and historians. John C. Miller's contribution to the New American Nation Series, *The Federalist Era, 1789-1801* (New York, 1960), is exhaustively researched, balanced, and an excellent synthesis. The period after 1801 has long been dominated by Henry Adams's *History of the United States during the Administration of Thomas Jefferson and James Madison* (9 vols., New York, 1889-91). The work is brilliant but prejudiced, and no extended corrective treatment has yet appeared. David Fischer, *The Revolution of American Conservatism* (New York, 1965) suggests an entirely new view of the Federalist party after 1801.

Charles Beard's writings on the Constitution and Federalist period, *An Economic Interpretation of the Constitution* (New York, 1913) and *Economic Origins of Jeffersonian Democracy* (New York, 1915), continue to stimulate scholarly controversy. His contemporary followers, who have modified but supported his thesis of American party warfare and development, range from Merrill Jensen, *The New Nation: A History of the United States During the Confederacy, 1781-1789* (New York, 1950), to Jackson T. Main, *The Anti-Federalists: Critics of the Constitution, 1781-1788* (Chapel Hill, 1961), to Manning Dauer, *The Adams Federalists* (Baltimore, 1953). Beard's work on the Constitution has been subjected to searing criticism by Robert E. Brown, *Charles Beard and the Constitution* (Princeton, 1956), and Forrest McDonald, *We the People: The Economic Origins of the Constitution* (Chicago, 1958). Historical journals in the past decade contain numerous articles and reviews expounding pro- and anti-Beardian views. Beard's work contains an appreciation of Hamiltonianism, but the new conservatism in America has given birth to more sophisticated analyses and appreciations of our first Secretary of the Treasury. The most recent is by Clinton Rossiter, *Alexander Hamilton and the Constitution* (New York, 1964). See also Rossiter's floridly written *1787: The Grand Convention* (New York, 1966). Antidotes can be found in Joseph Charles's provocative little book, *The Origins of the American Party System* (Williamsburg, 1956) and in the fascinating detective work on Hamilton's intrigues by Julian Boyd, *Number 7: Alexander Hamilton's Secret Attempts to Control American Foreign Policy* (Princeton, 1964). Scholars cannot seem to escape identification with either Hamilton or Jefferson. "Alas," says Merrill Peterson, "it is inescapable."

James M. Smith has written the definitive study of the Alien and Sedition Acts, *Freedom's Fetters: The Alien and Sedition Laws and American Civil Liberties* (Ithaca, 1956). Mark De Wolfe Howe believes Smith errs in a major premise, that the Alien and Sedition Acts were unconstitutional. A comparable volume on the Kentucky and Virginia Resolutions is yet to be written, though Harry Ammons and Adrienne Koch have contributed a significant essay on the subject. This essay is incorporated in the volume by Koch, *Jefferson and Madison: The Great Collaboration* (New York, 1950). The best work in the field of administrative history of the early national era is that of Leonard White, *The Federalists* (New York, 1948) and *The Jeffersonians, 1801-1829* (New York, 1951). Political historians dealing with economic subjects have sometimes stumbled, and it is generally preferable to reverse the process and have a non-professional scholar, trained in finance, with a fluid pen and keen mind, utilize his knowledge in the field of history. Bray Hammond fits this description. His volume *Banks and Politics in America from the Revolution to the Civil War* (Princeton, 1957) is indispensable for an understanding of the interrelationships of banking and politics. The formation and growth of the Republican party has been detailed (some critics say too much detail and not enough analysis) by Noble Cunningham in two volumes, *The Jeffersonian Republicans: The Formation of Party Organization, 1789-1801* (Chapel Hill, 1957) and *The Jeffersonian Republicans in Power: Party Operations, 1801-1809* (Chapel Hill, 1963). Norman Risjord deals with the conservative wing of the Republican party in *The Old Republicans* (New York, 1965).

The standard works on the Jay and Pinckney treaties are by Samuel F. Bemis, *Jay's Treaty: A Study in Commerce and Diplo-*

macy (New York, 1923) and *Pinckney's Treaty: A Study of America's Advantage from Europe's Distress* (Baltimore, 1926). French-American relations during Washington's administration are covered in Alexander De Conde, *Entangling Alliance: Politics and Diplomacy under George Washington* (Durham, 1958). A sequel by De Conde, to be published, will deal with French-American relations through the Adams administration. Spanish-American relations are treated most thoroughly by Arthur Whitaker in *The Spanish-American Frontier: 1783-1795* (Boston, 1927) and *The Mississippi Question, 1795-1803* (New York, 1934). Anglo-American relations after 1795 are contained in two volumes by Bradford Perkins, *The First Rapprochement: England and the United States, 1795-1805* (Philadelphia, 1953) and *Prologue to War: England and the United States, 1805-1812* (Berkeley, 1961). Both volumes have received considerable acclaim. The literature of foreign relations on the coming and causes of the War of 1812 continues to mount, an ever-increasing historiographical burden for the student. See, for example, Reginald Horsman, *The Causes of the War of 1812* (Philadelphia, 1962) and Roger Brown, *The Republic in Peril: 1812* (New York, 1964). A brief summary of the literature of causation, and of the war itself, is provided in Harry Coles's recent work, *The War of 1812* (Chicago, 1965). A monograph on the Hartford Convention is needed.

INDEX